# The Stress Relieving Coloring Book For Adults

Erin Sherriff

# THANK YOU FOR PURCHASING THIS BOOK

Each left hand page of this book has been left blank to avoid any bleed through of the page plus it provides you with a clear space to test out any shading that you want to use before actually applying it to the image your coloring.

As the owner of this book you are free to photocopy or scan and print out any of the pages in this book for your own, personal, use only. This does not give you permission to resell or use any of the images for commercial use or gain in any way. The images contained in this book remain the copyright of the publisher.

Experiment with shading, colors and light to produce the effect that makes the best of the images and your artistic skills. I hope that you enjoy this book as much as I did creating it.

 **Get a new coloring image each week for FREE**

Come and join our Facebook page for help, tips and advice about getting the best from your coloring. Each week we release a new, exclusive, image that you can download and print out. You'll also be the first to hear about new coloring books that we release along with special discounts.

Join us at https://www.facebook.com/**adults**coloring**books**/

*THIS BOOK BELONGS TO:*

_____

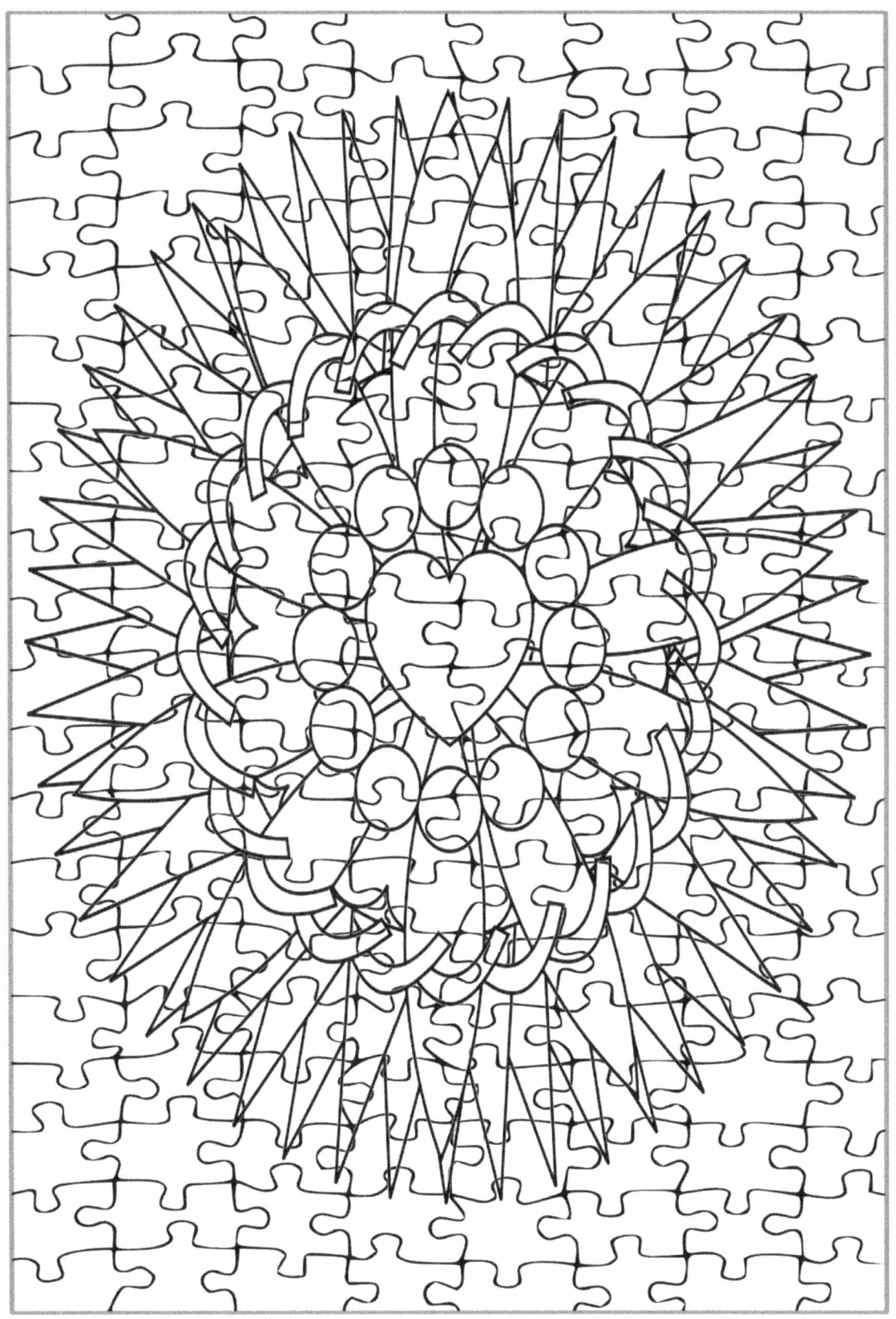

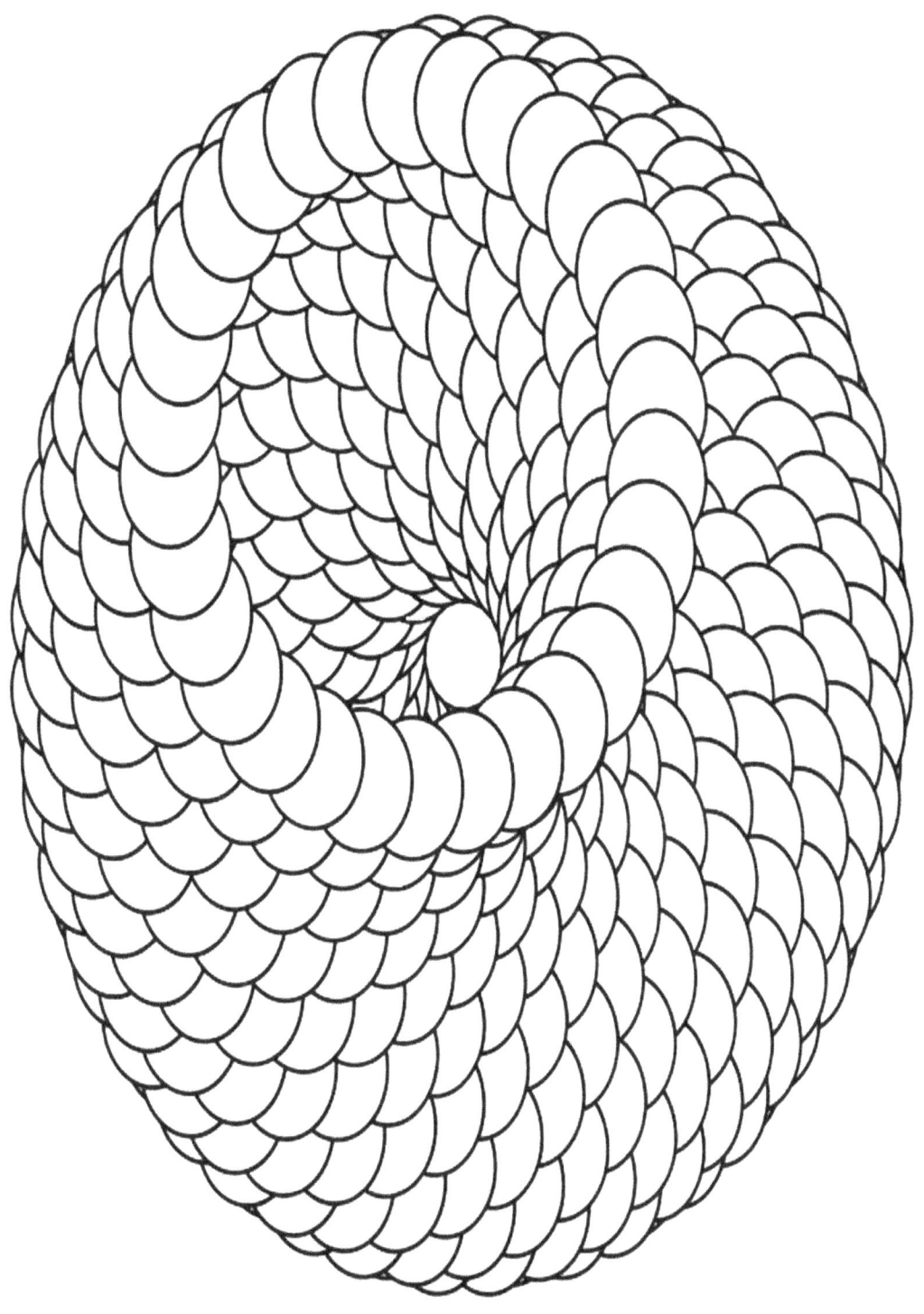

8

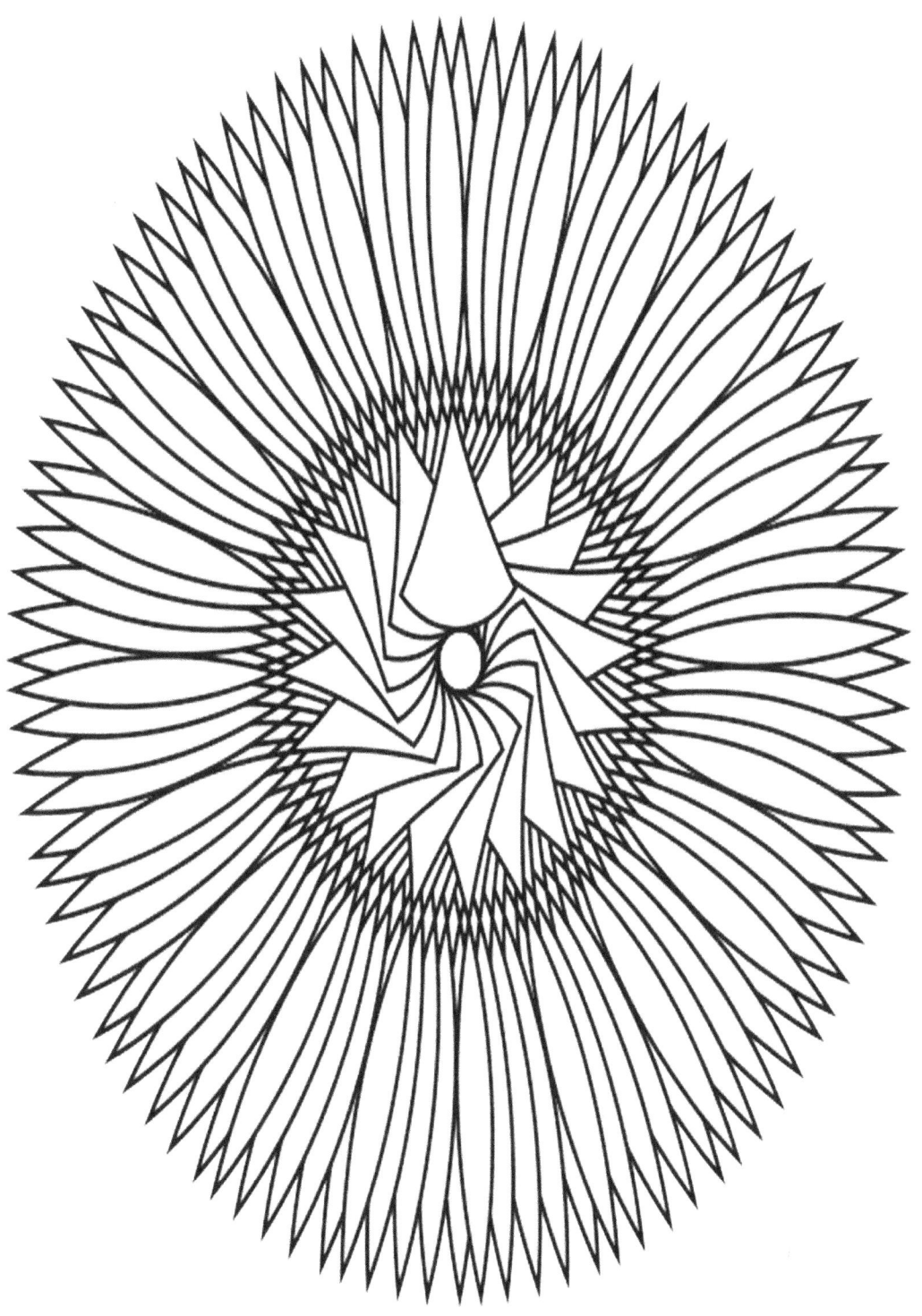

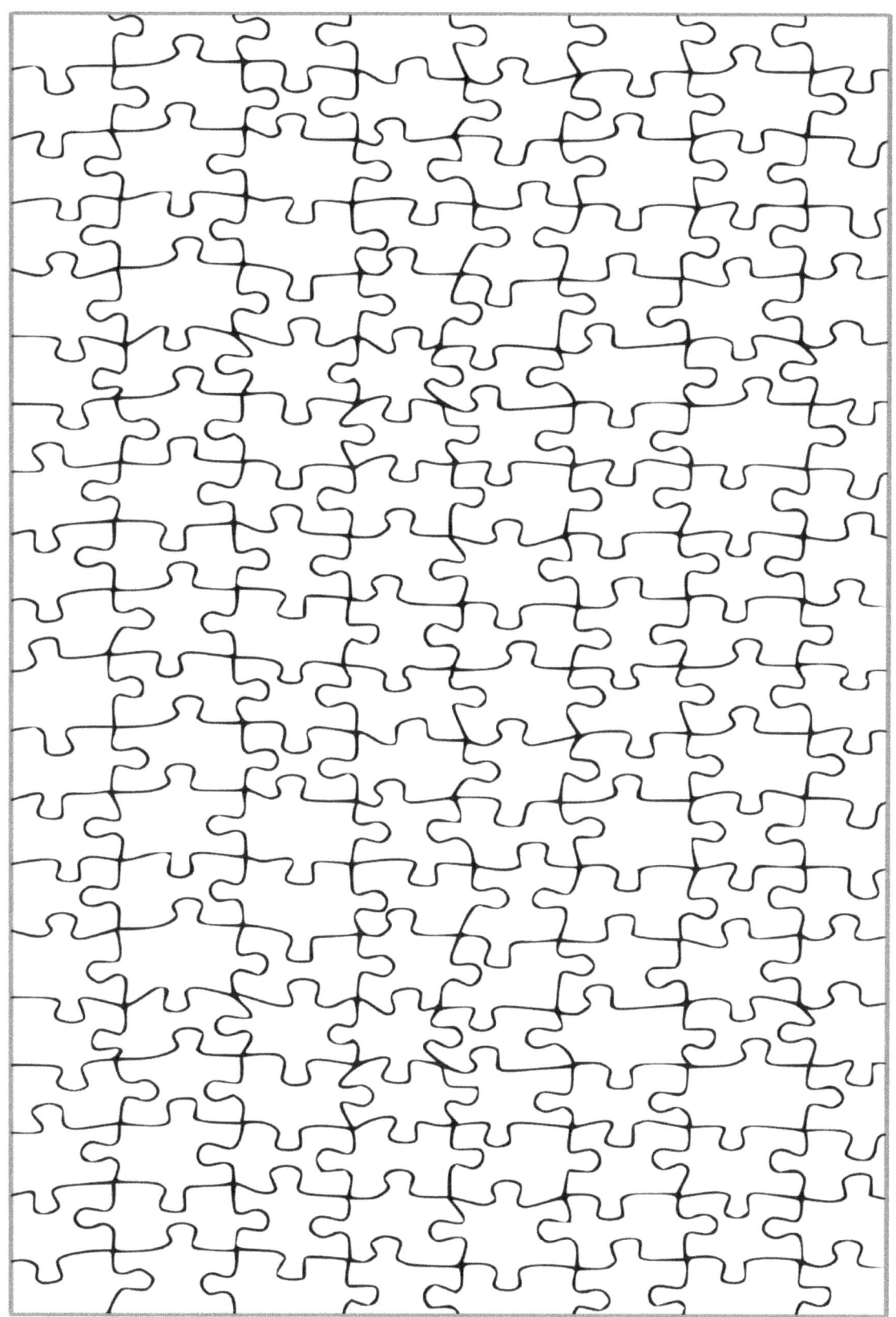

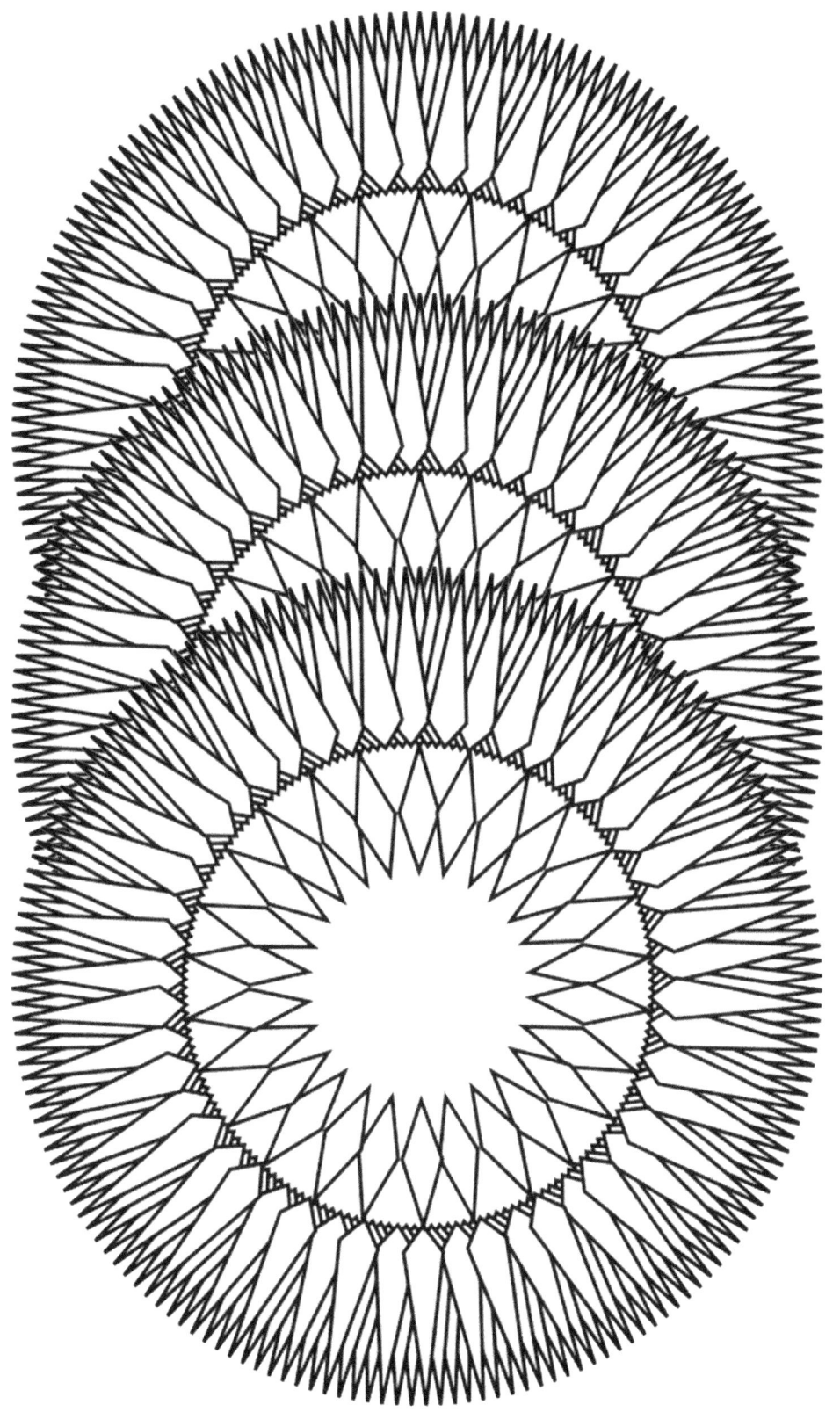

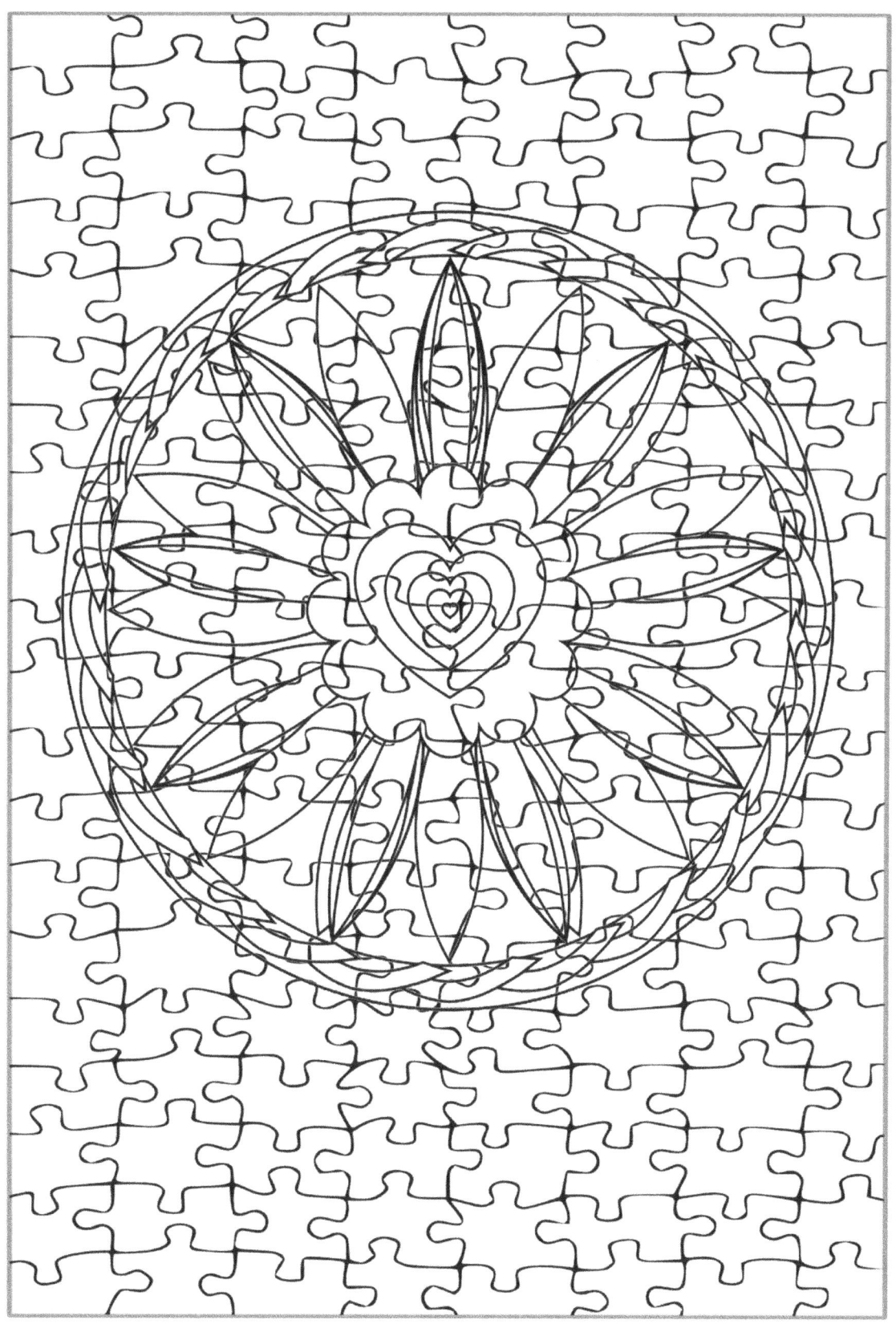

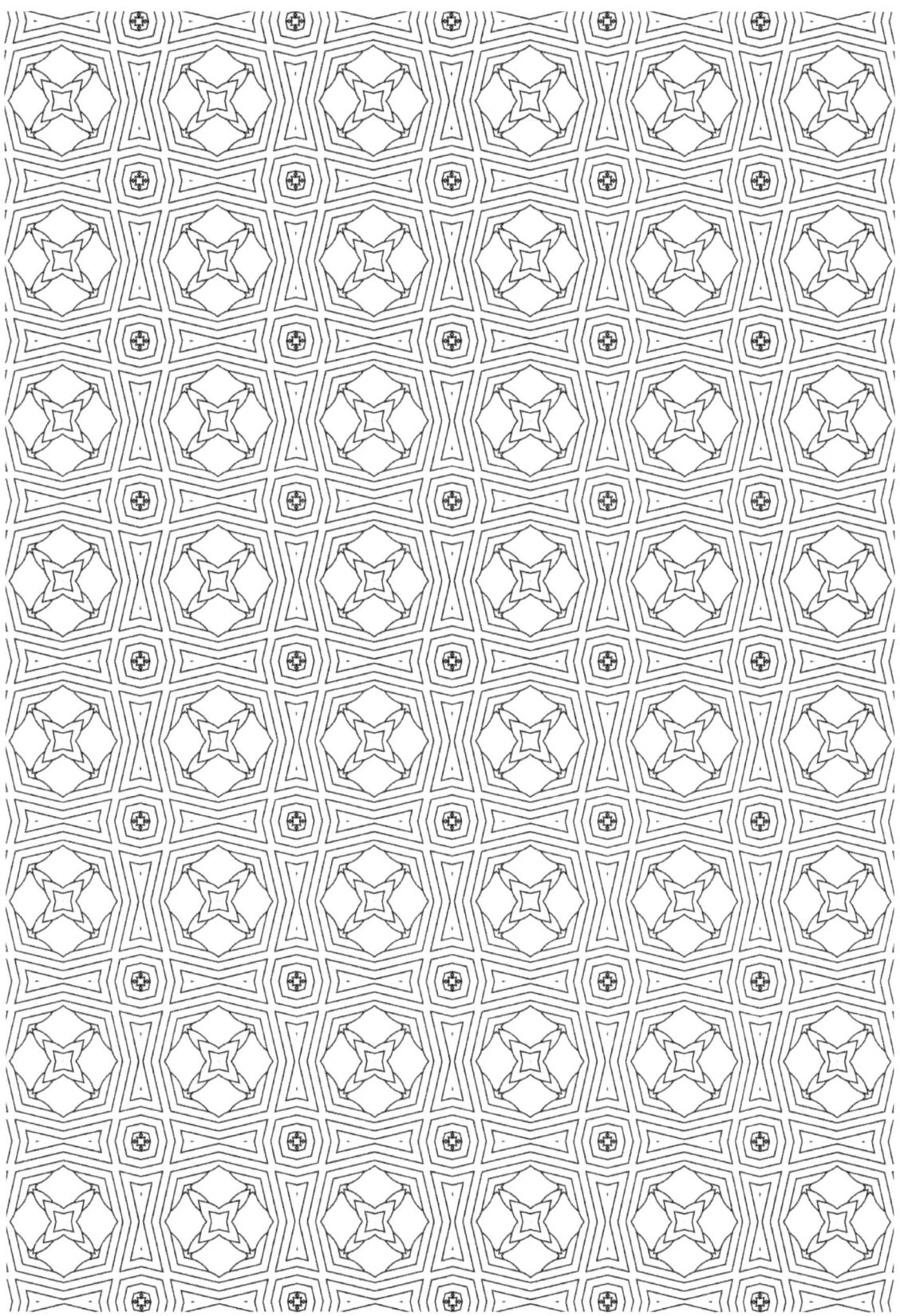

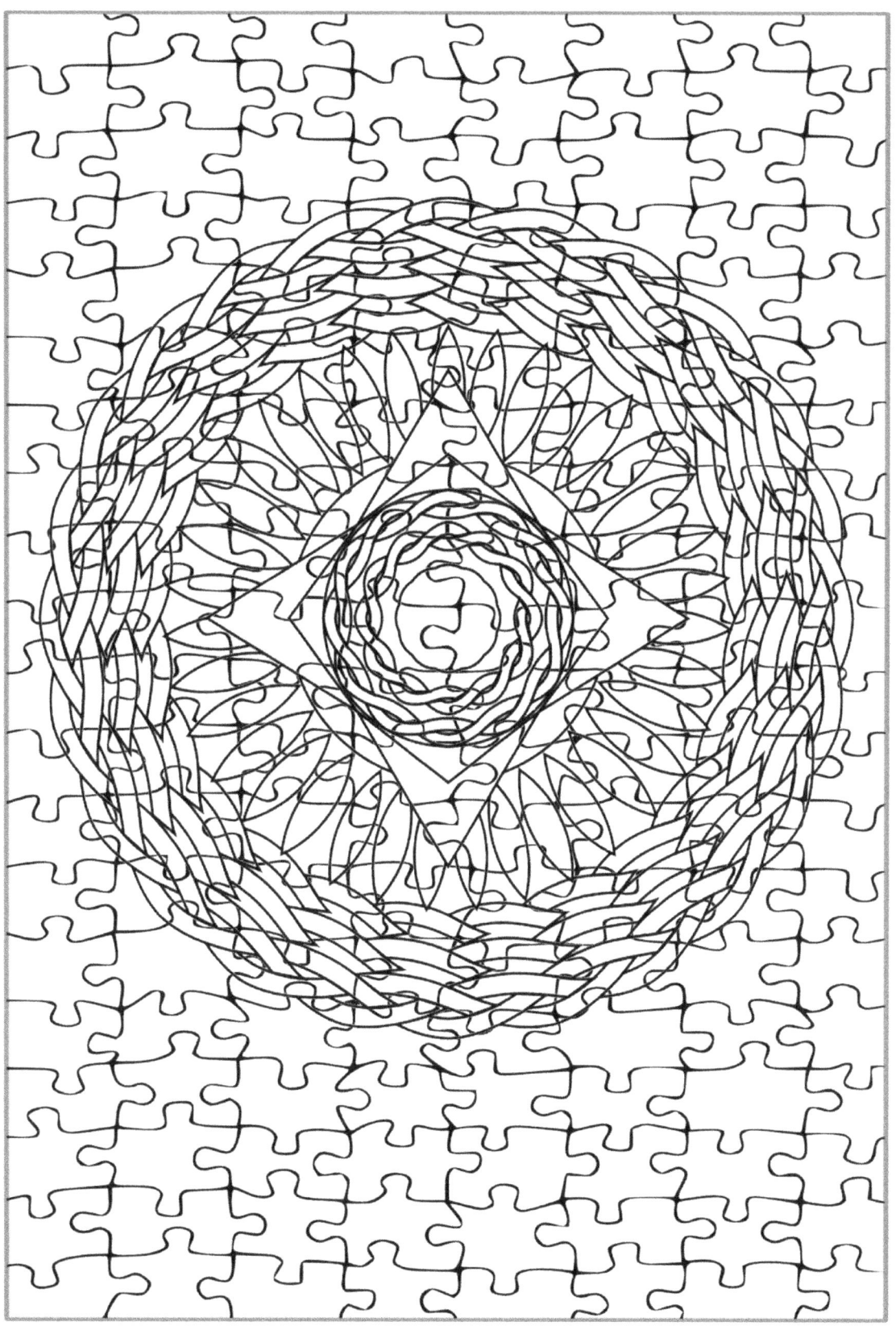

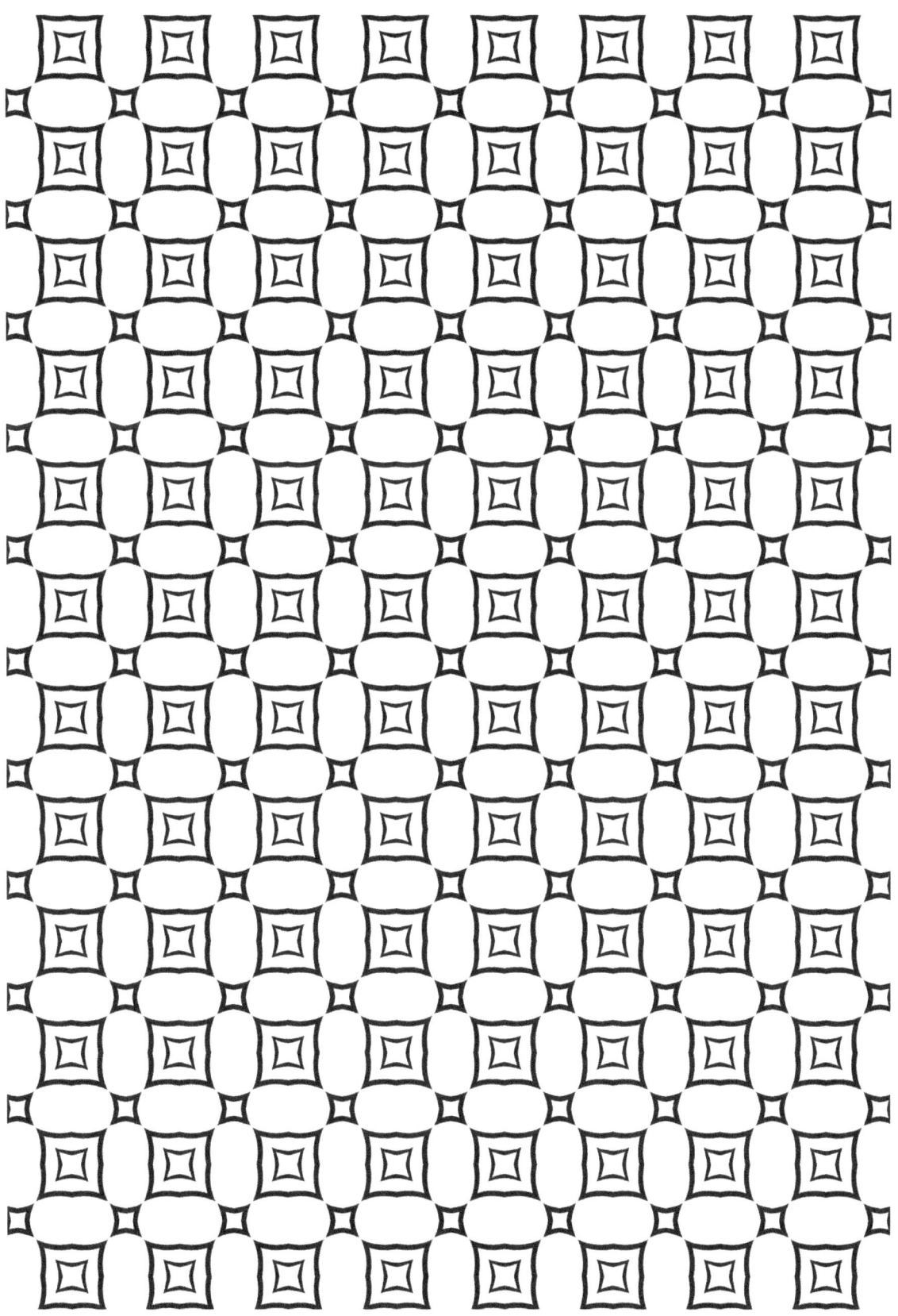

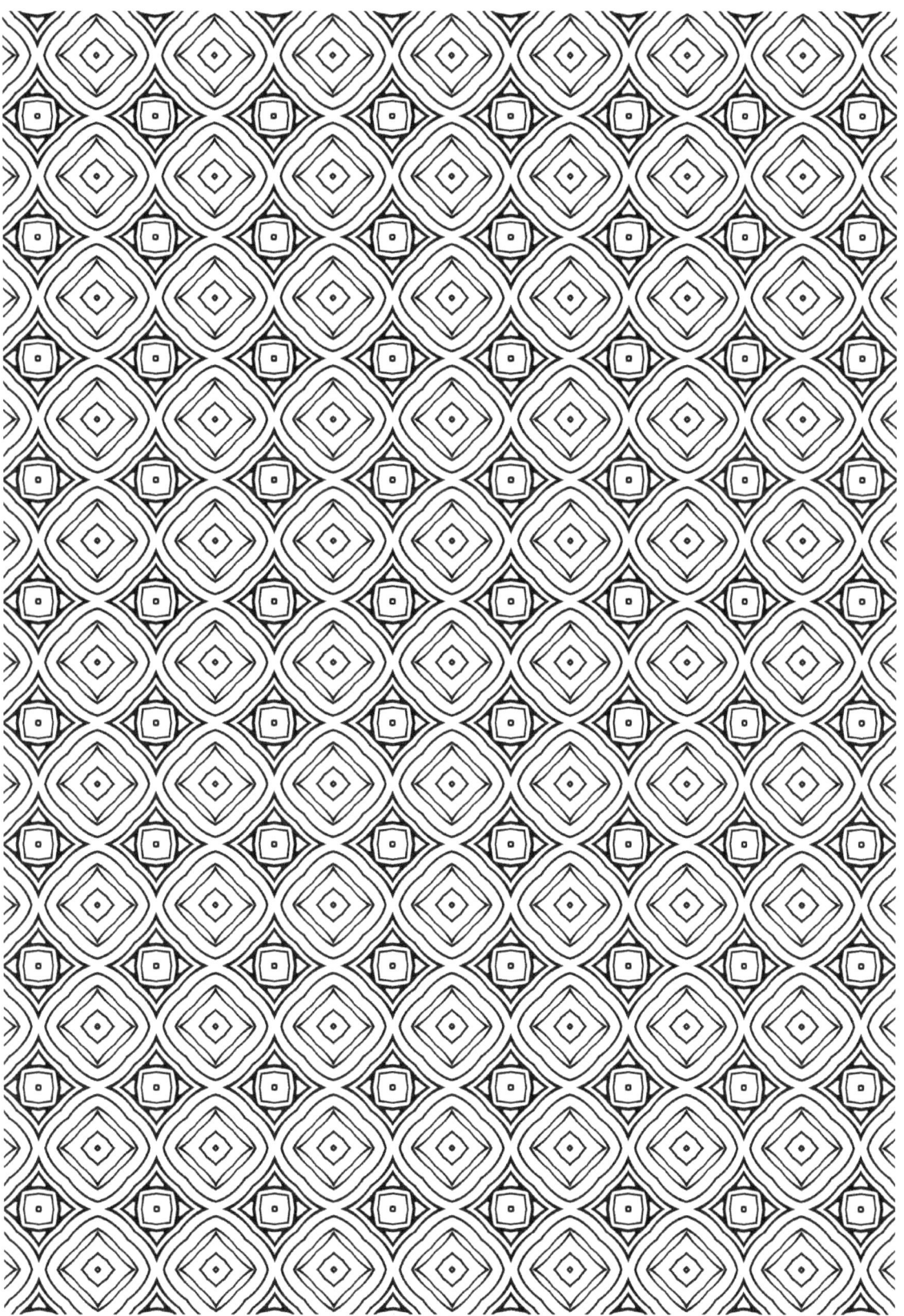

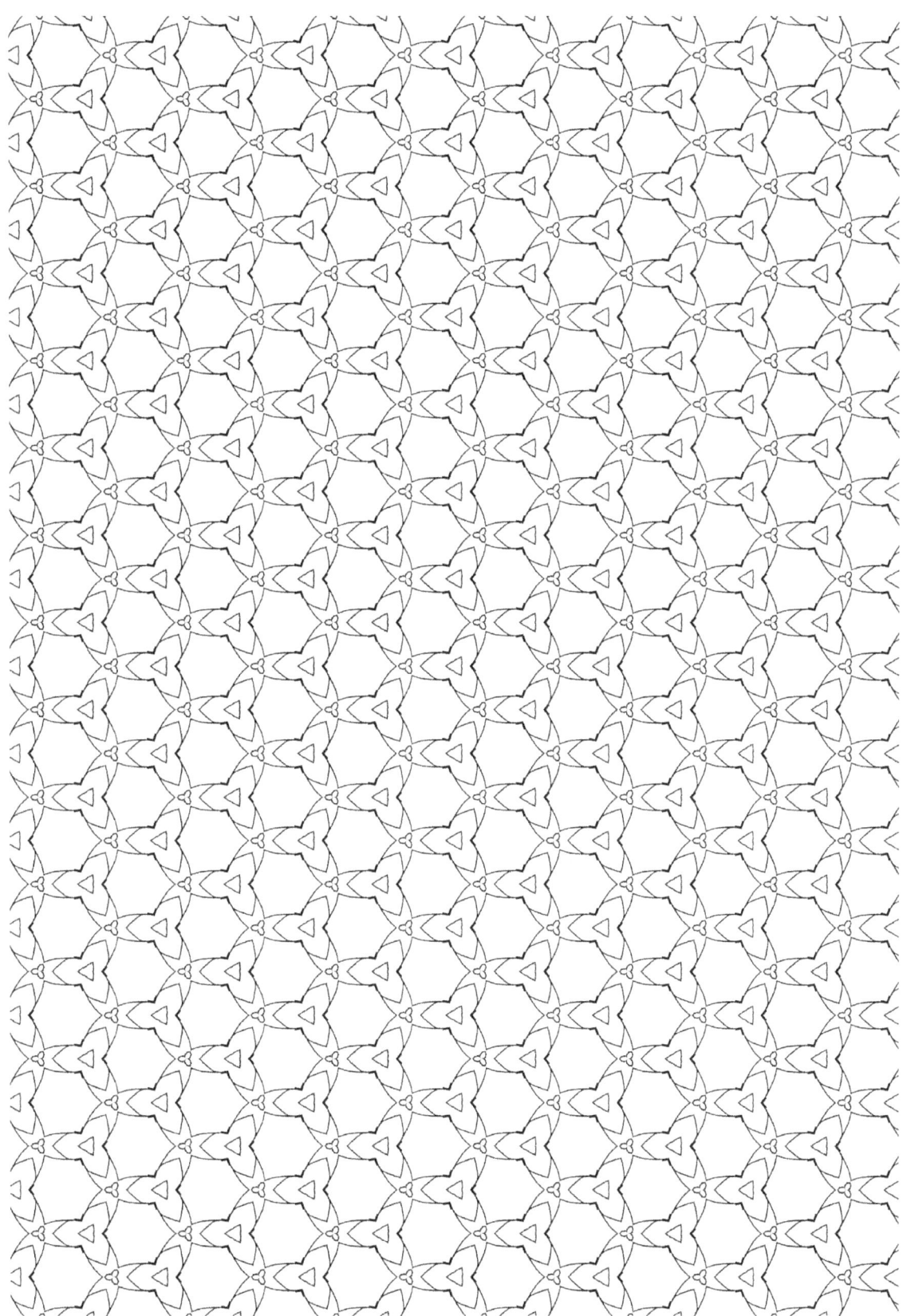

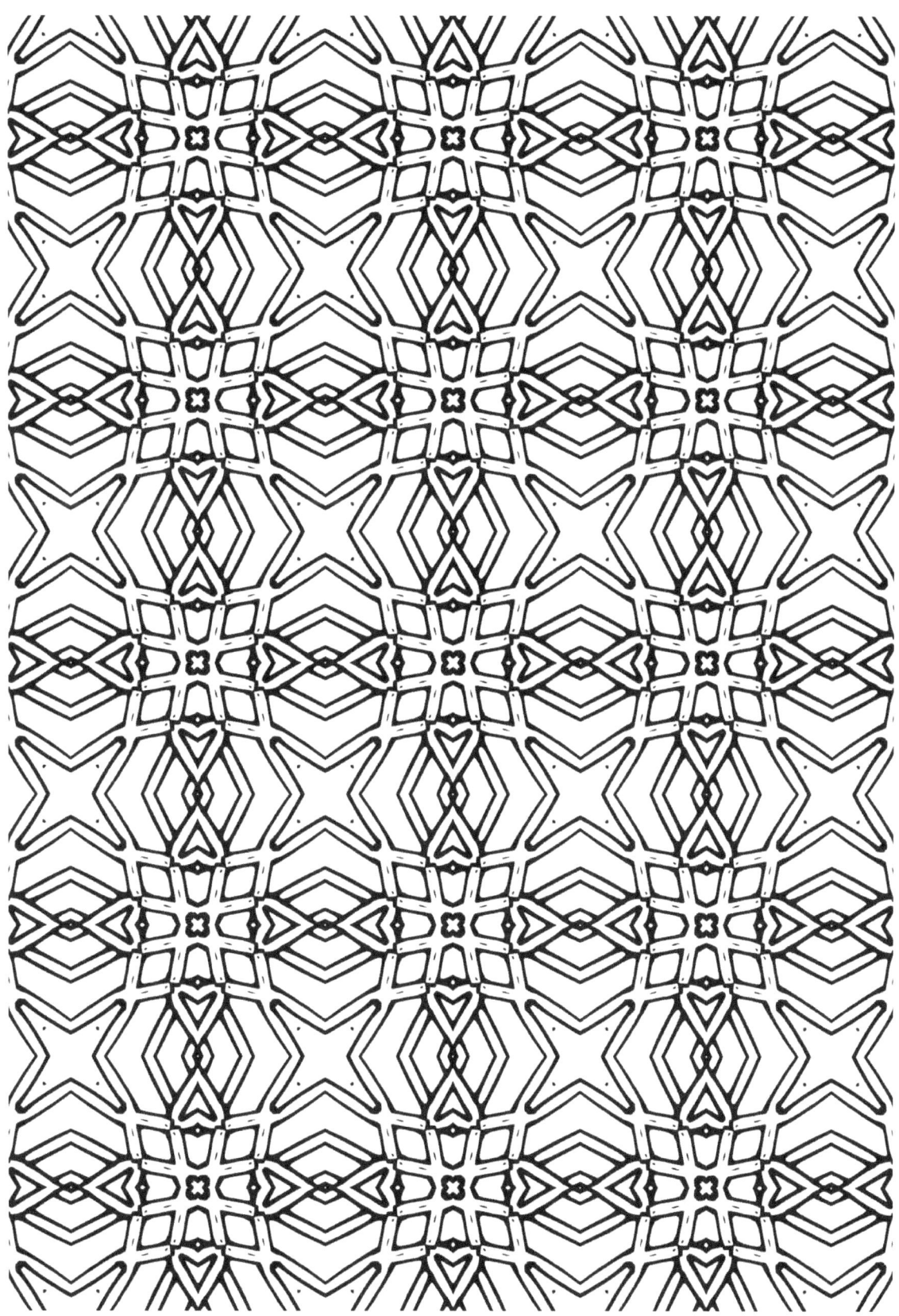

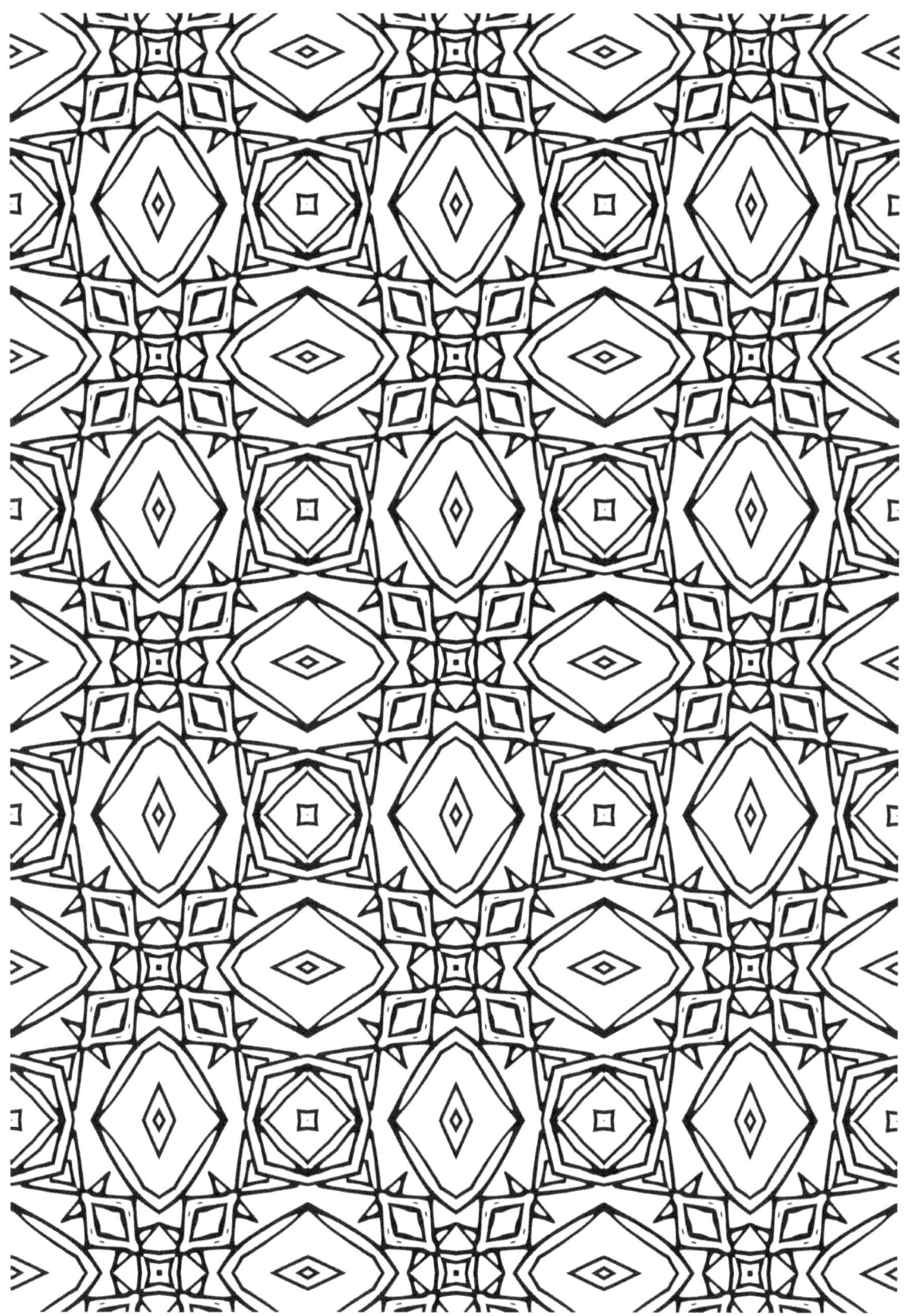

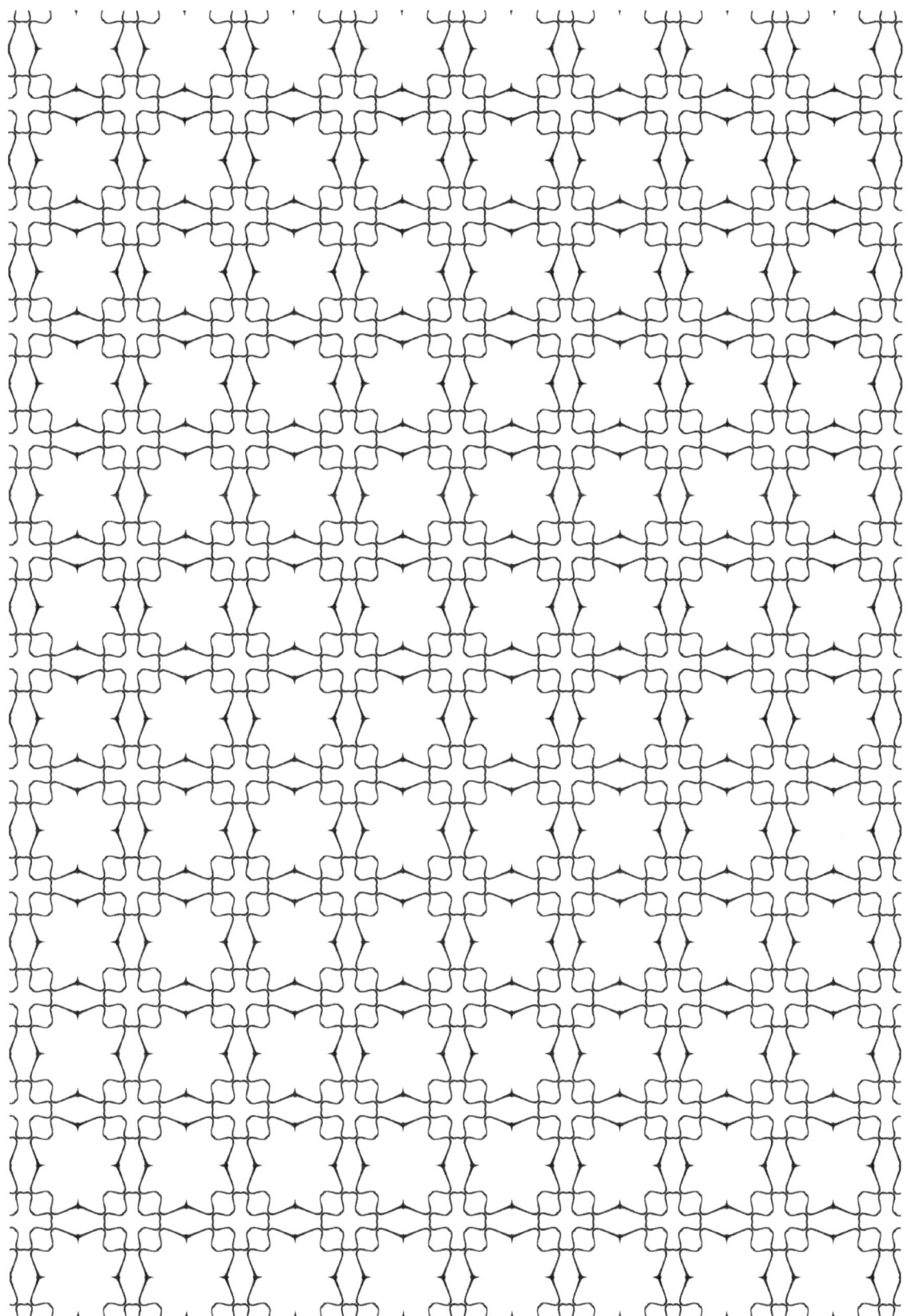

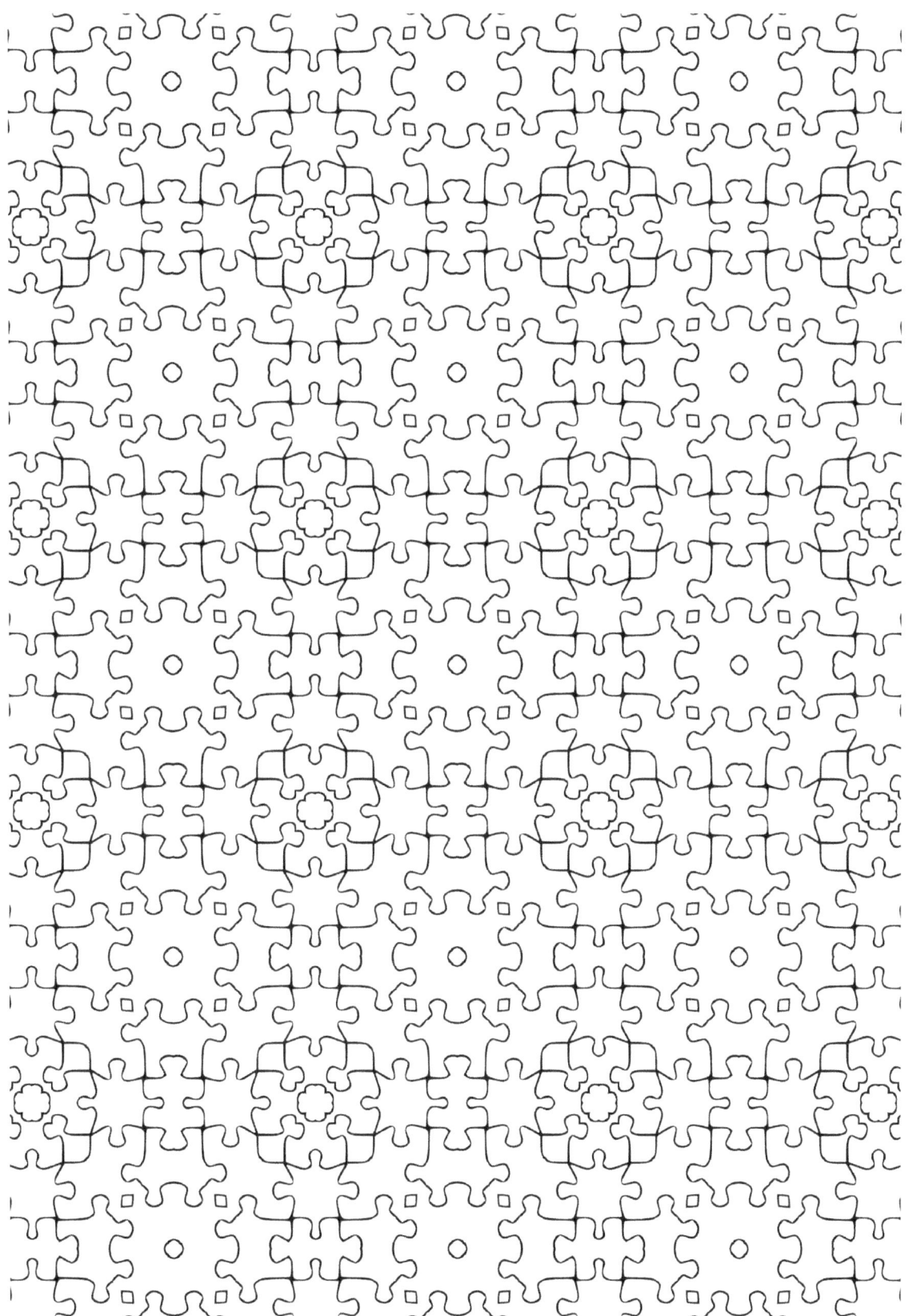

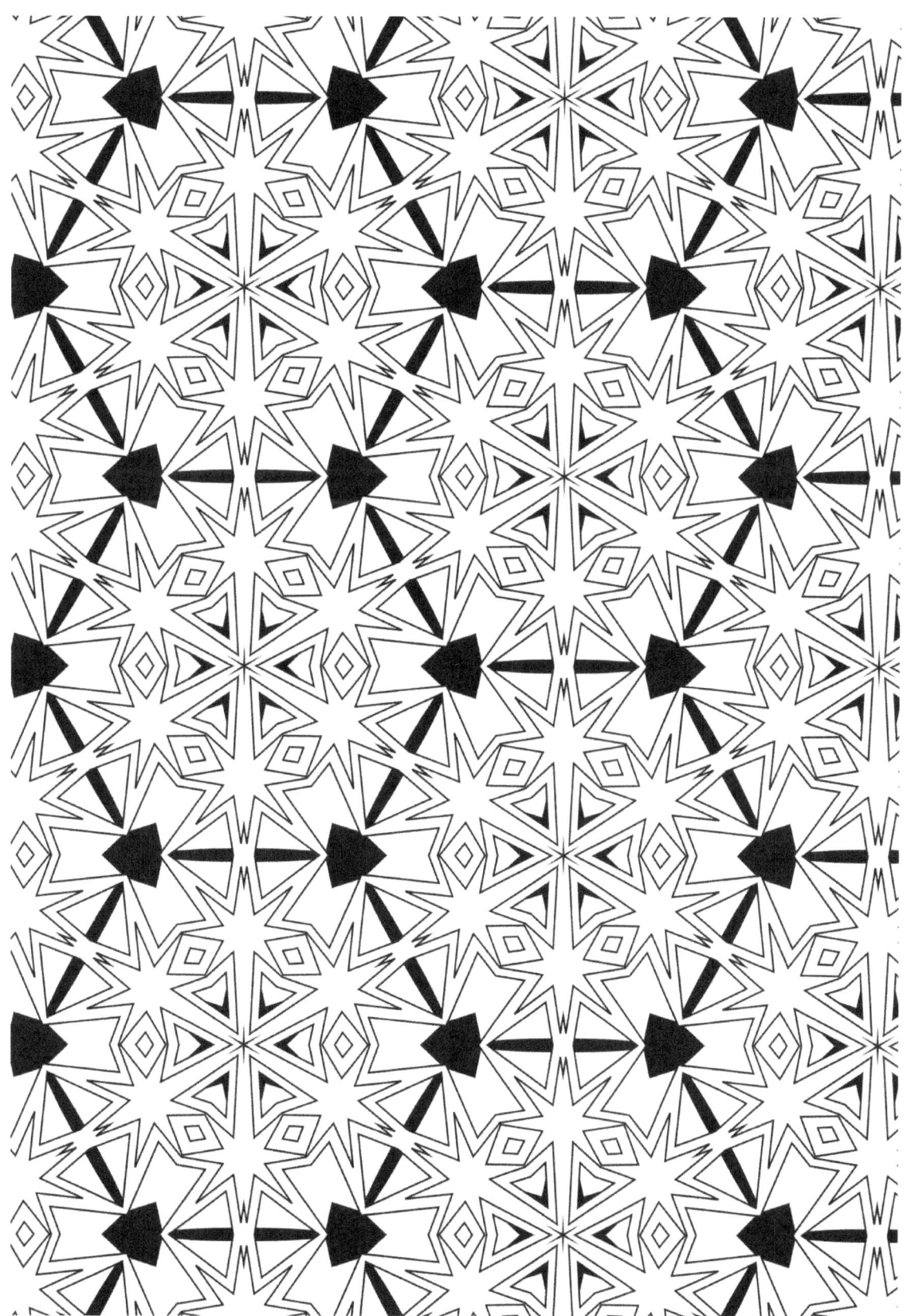

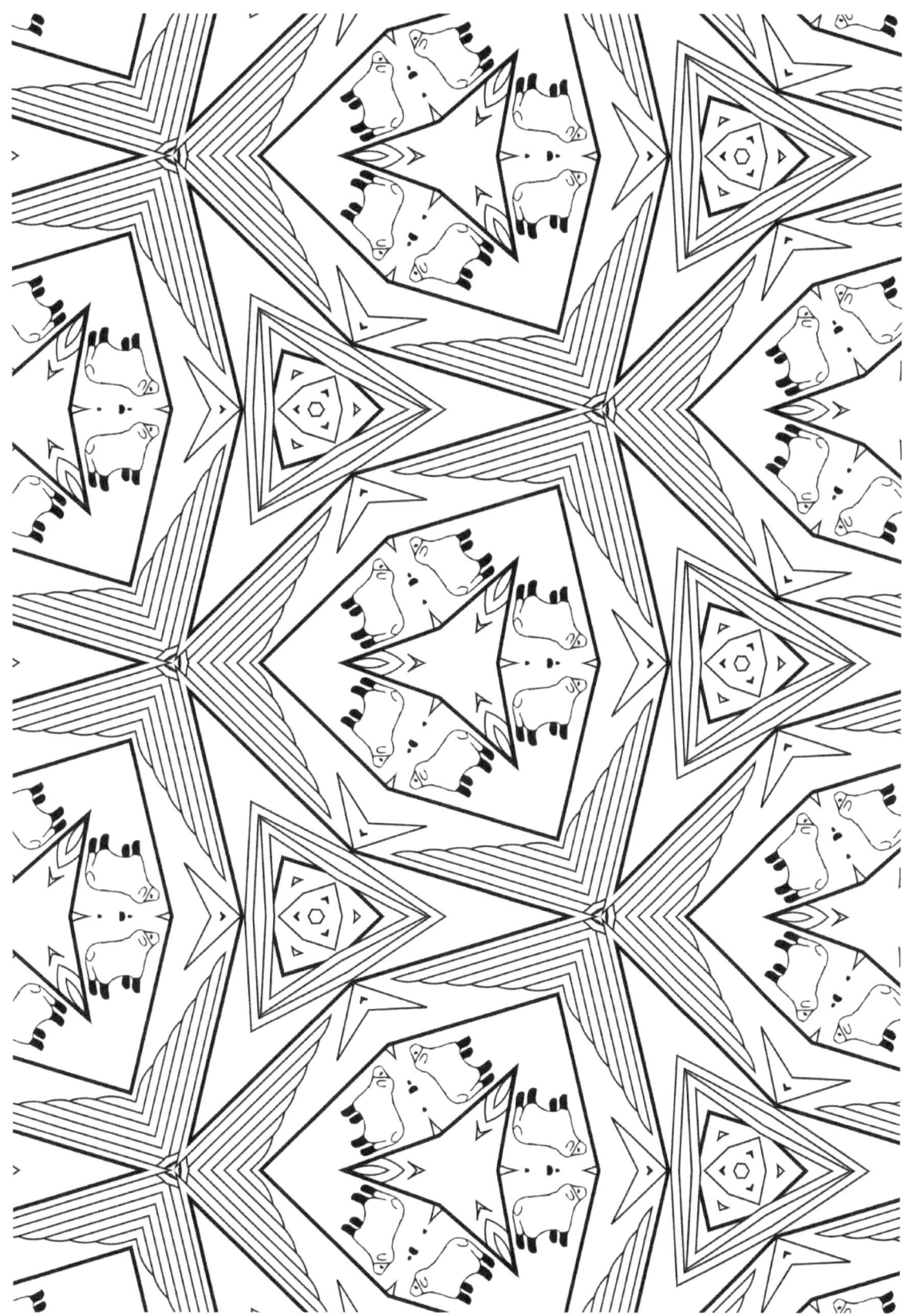

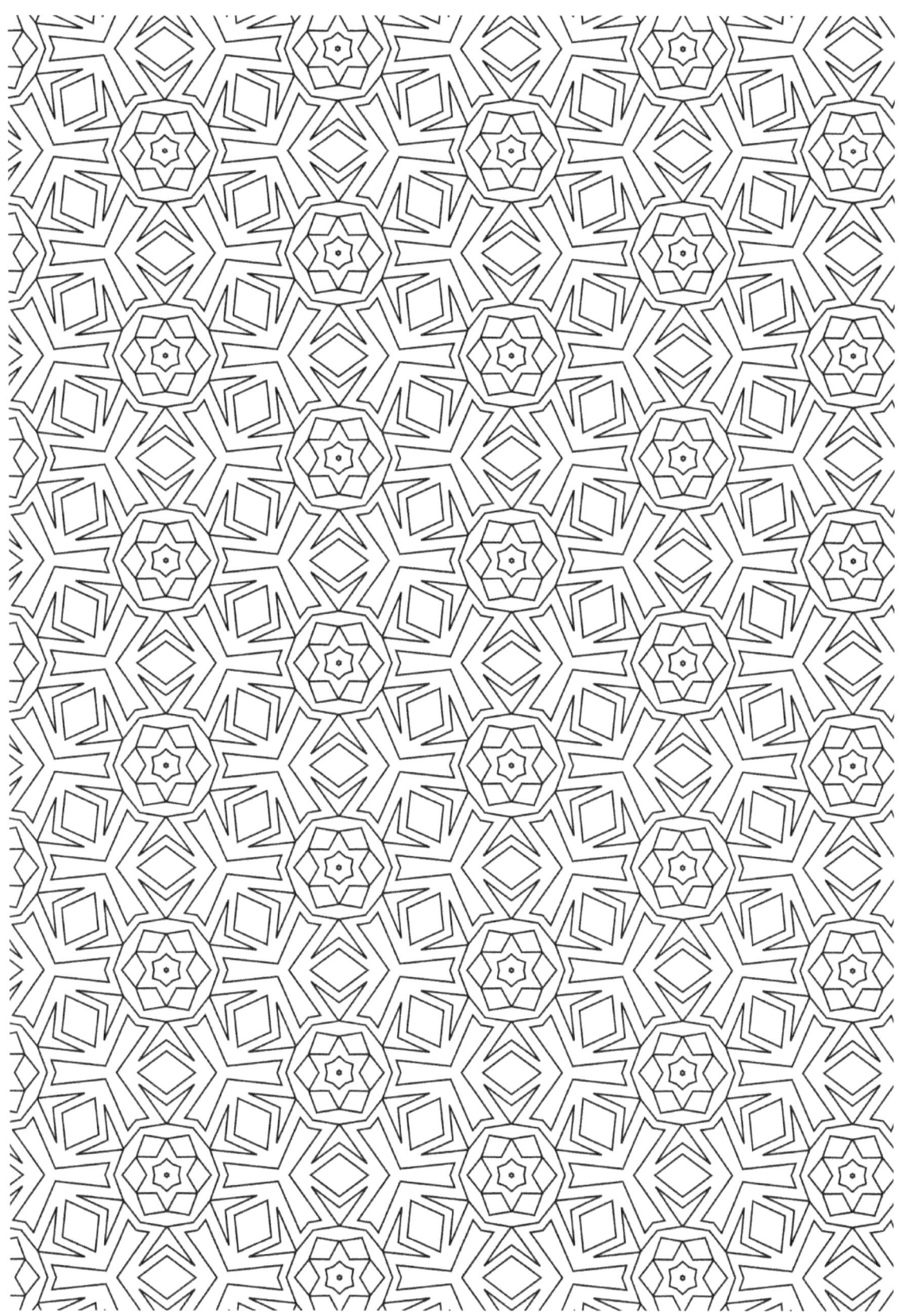

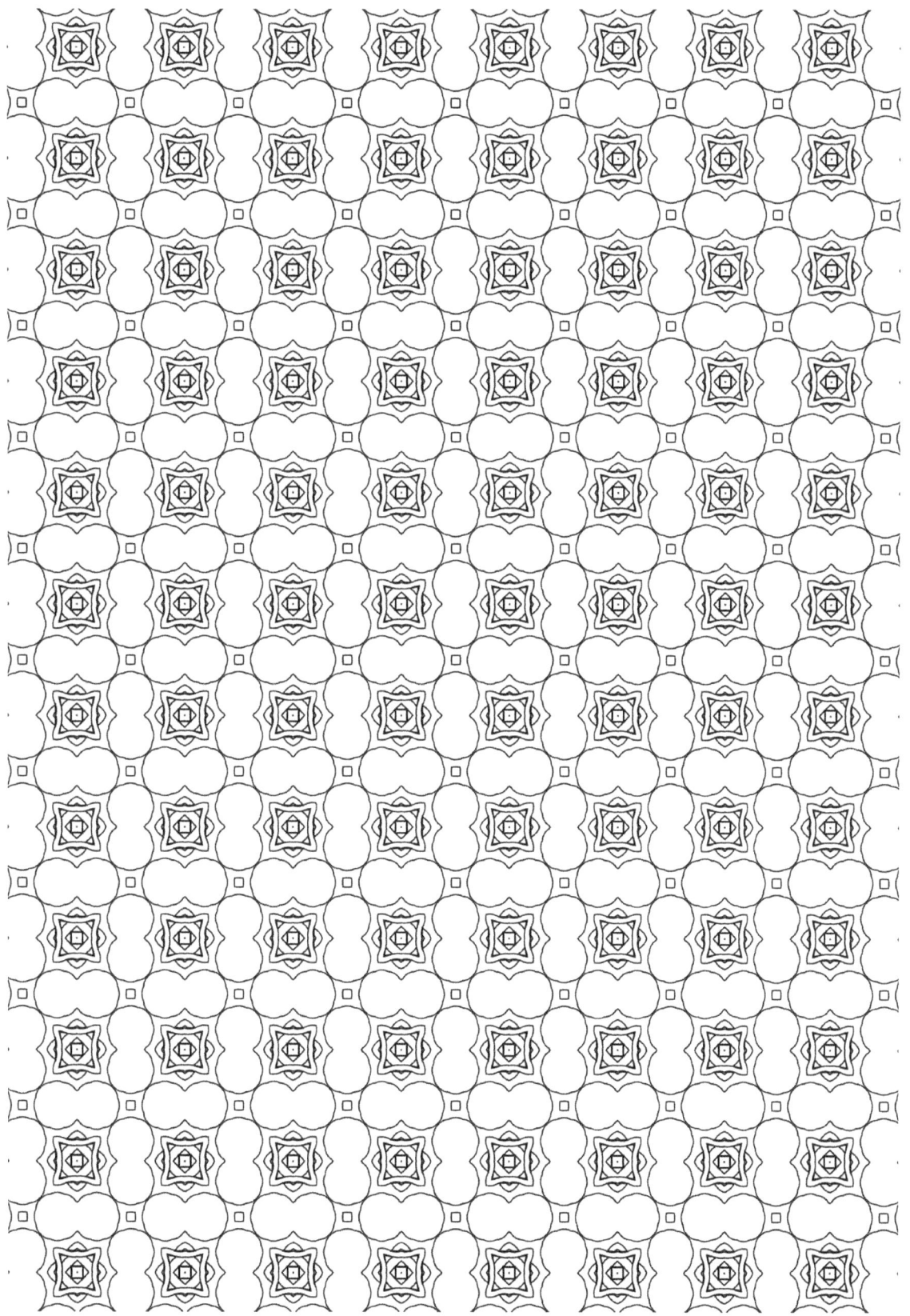

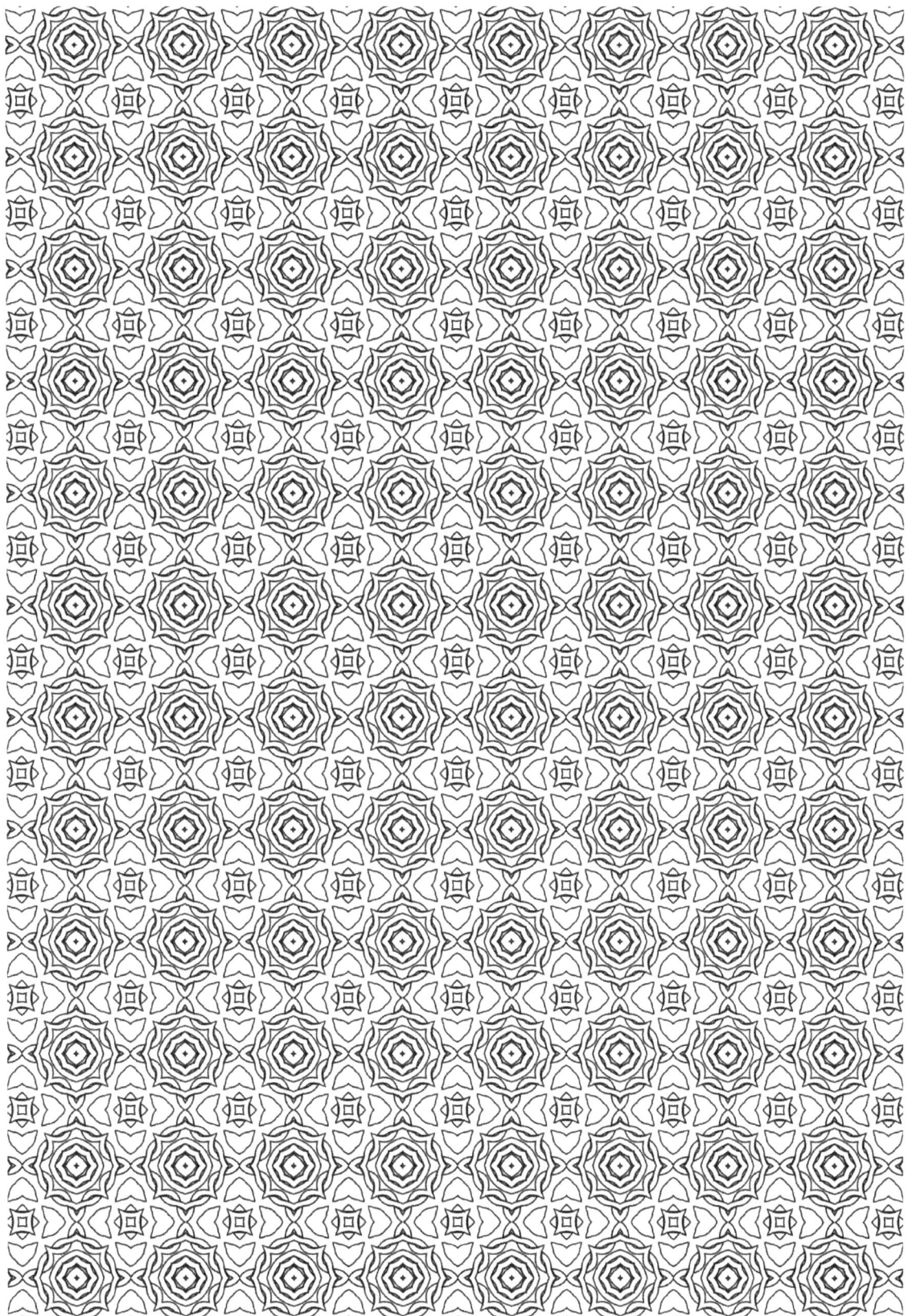

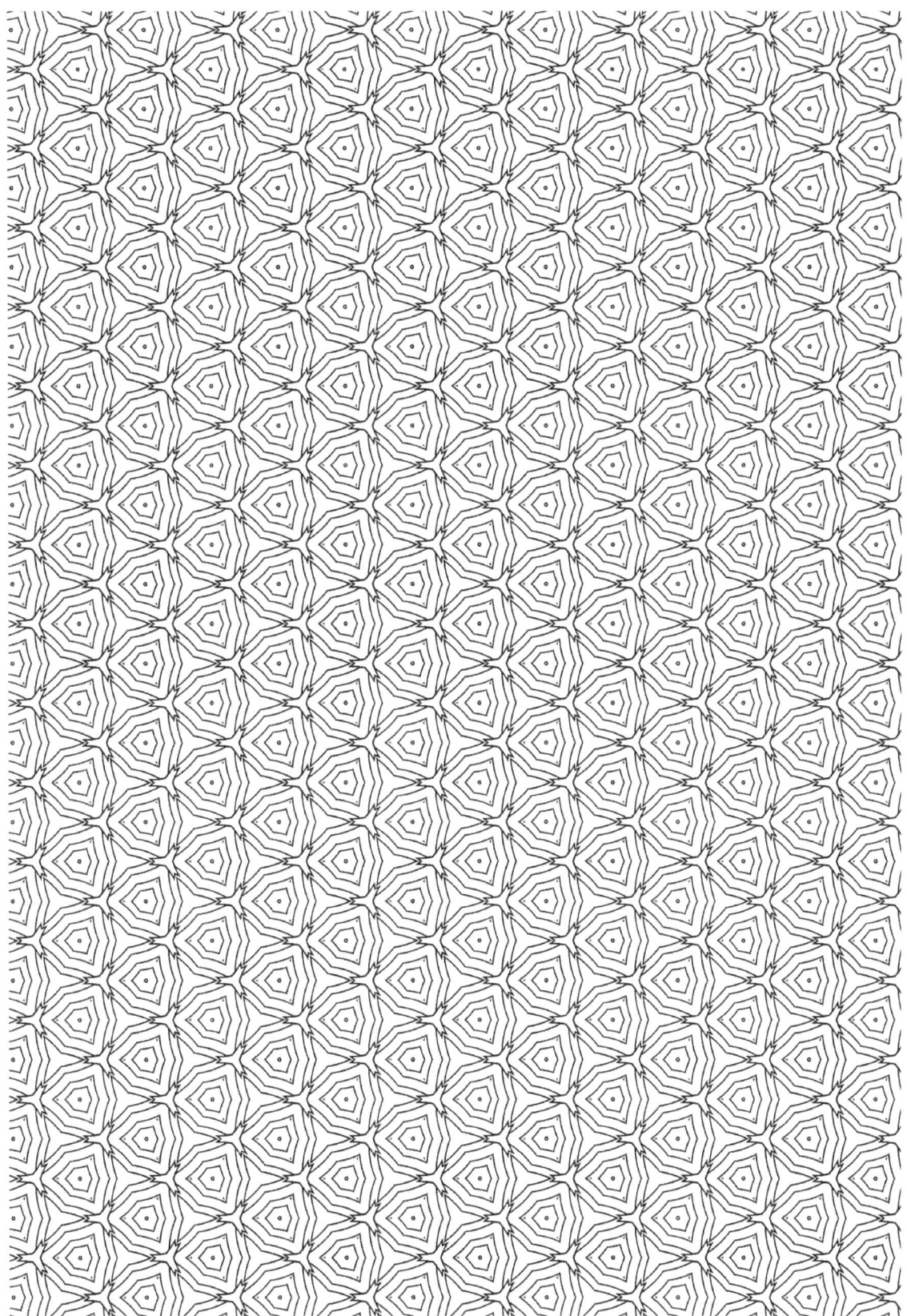

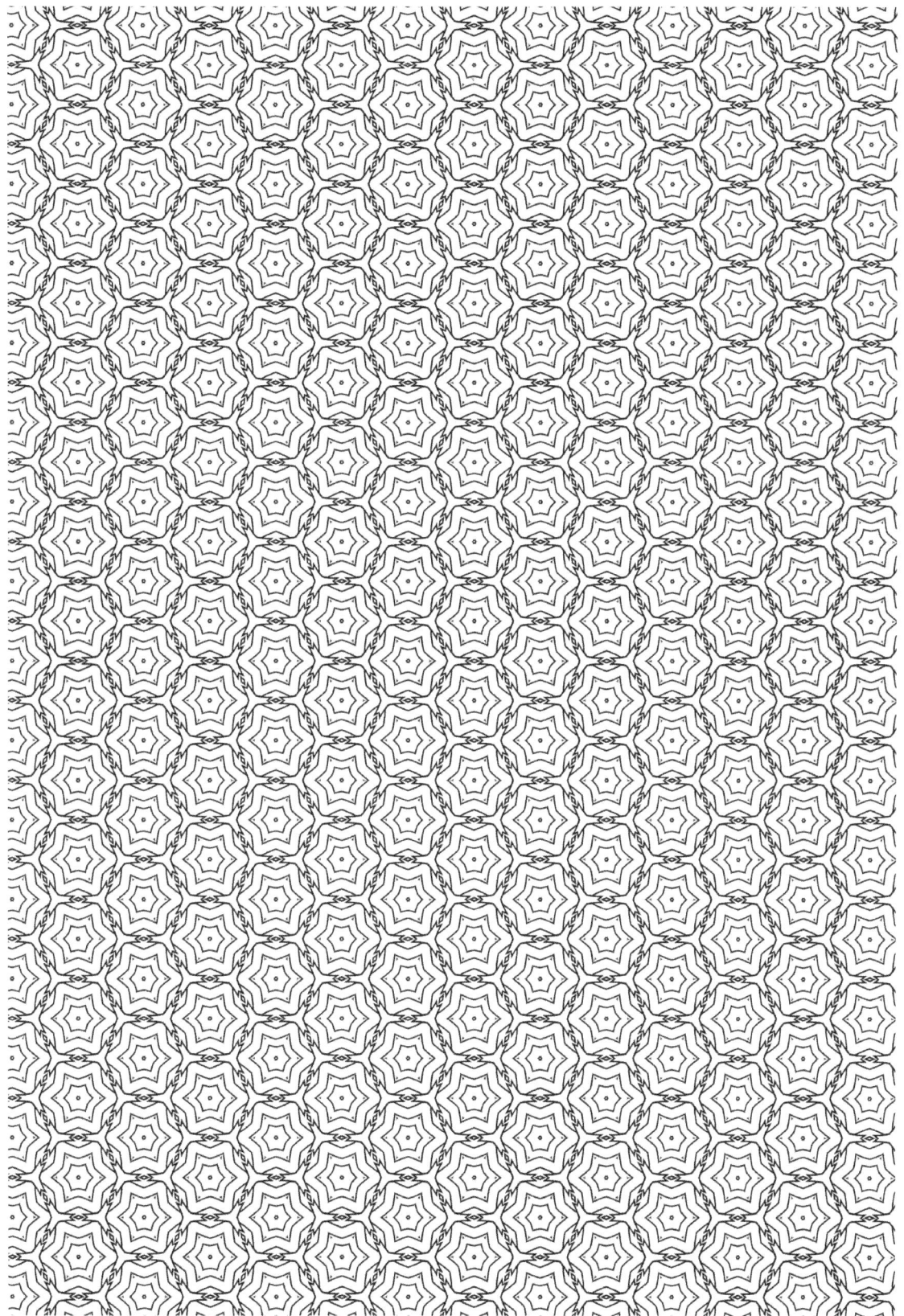

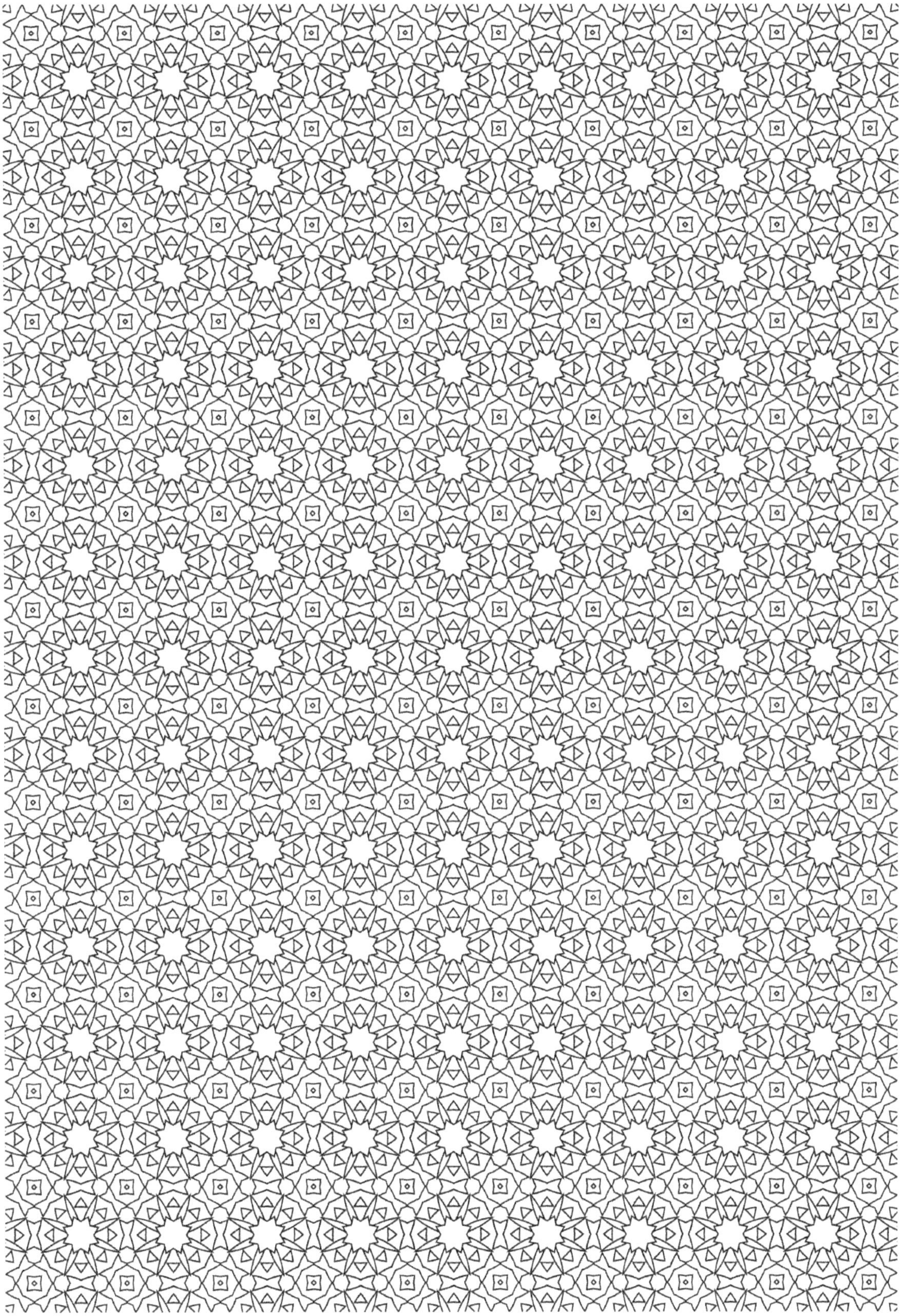

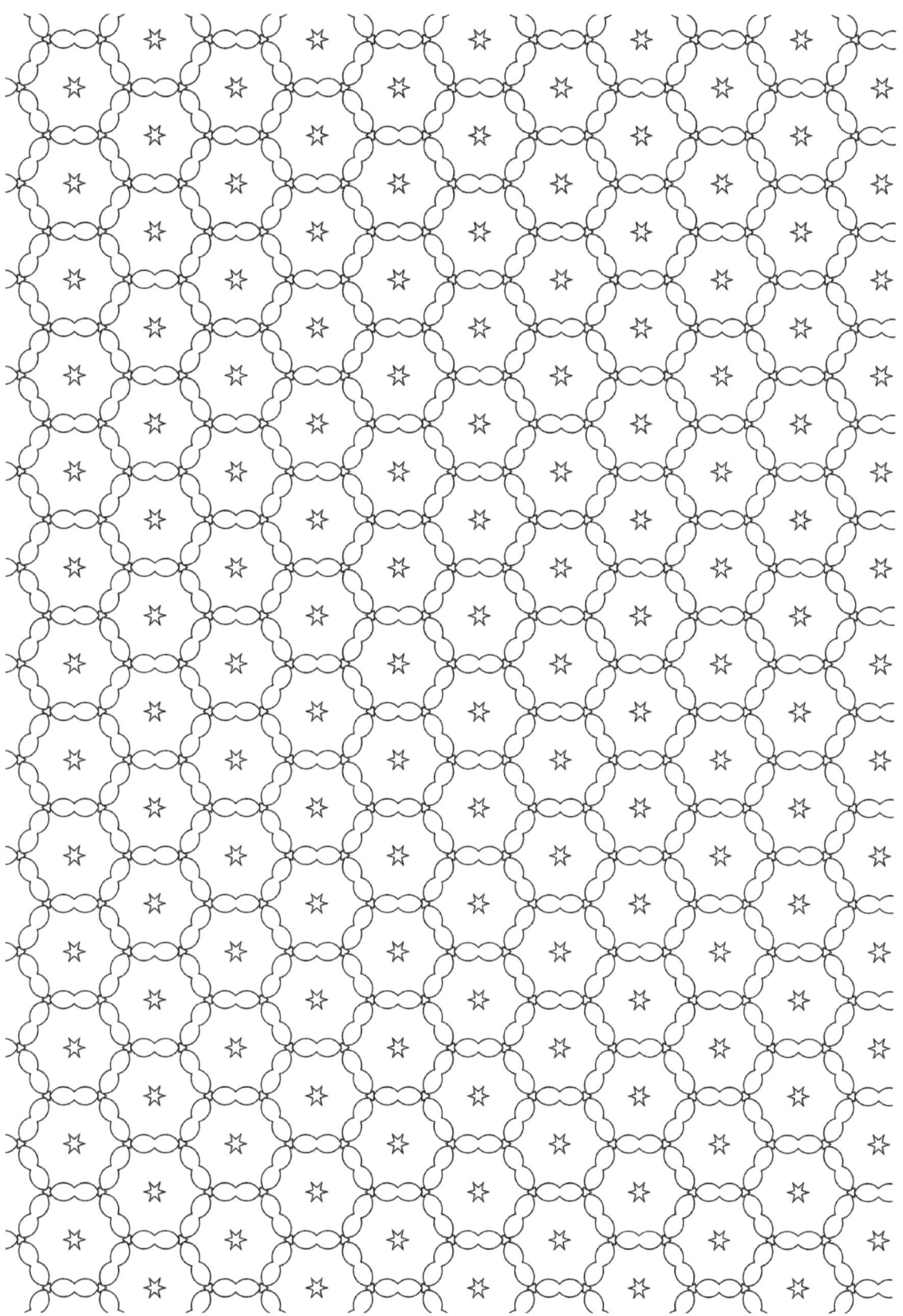

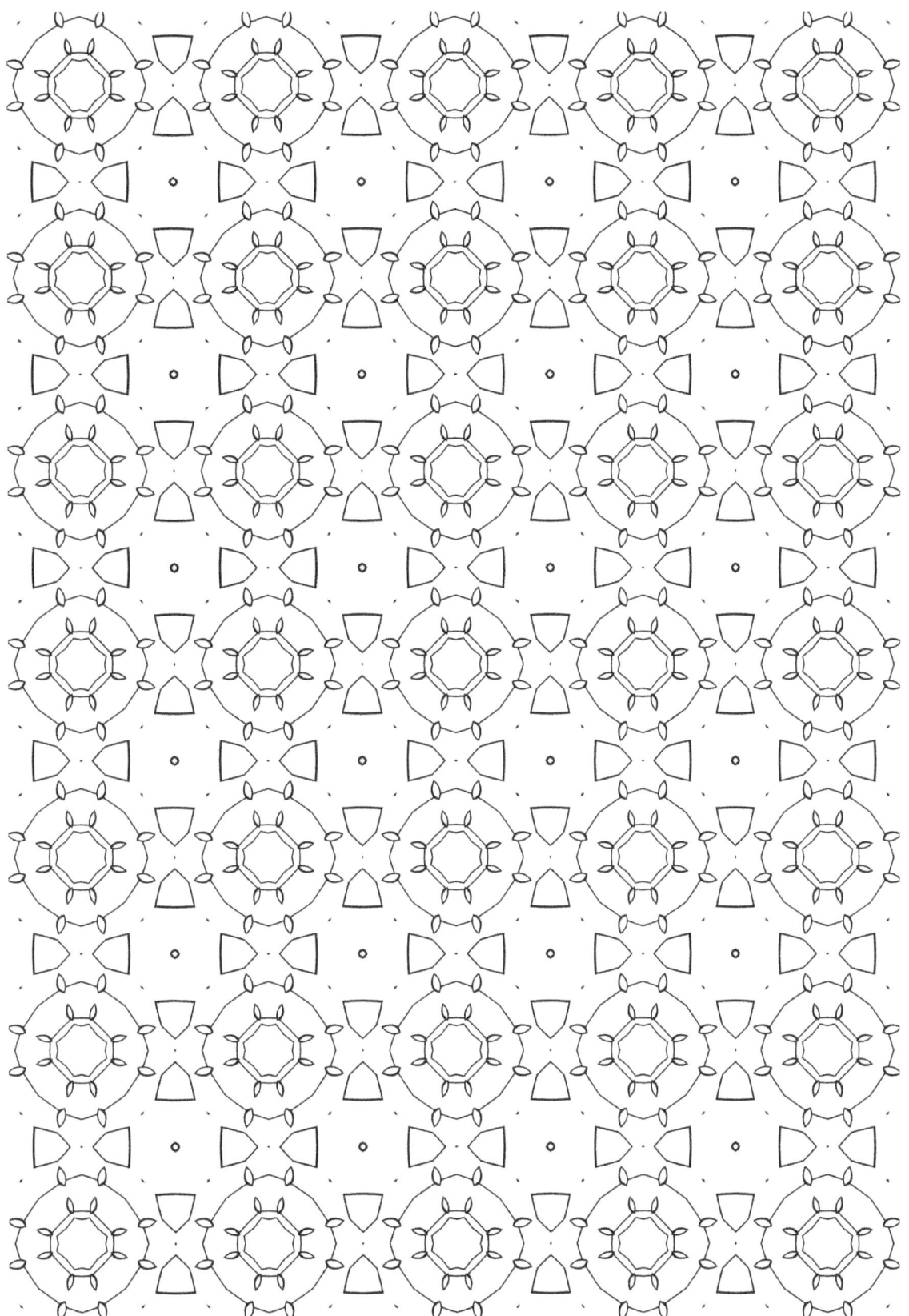

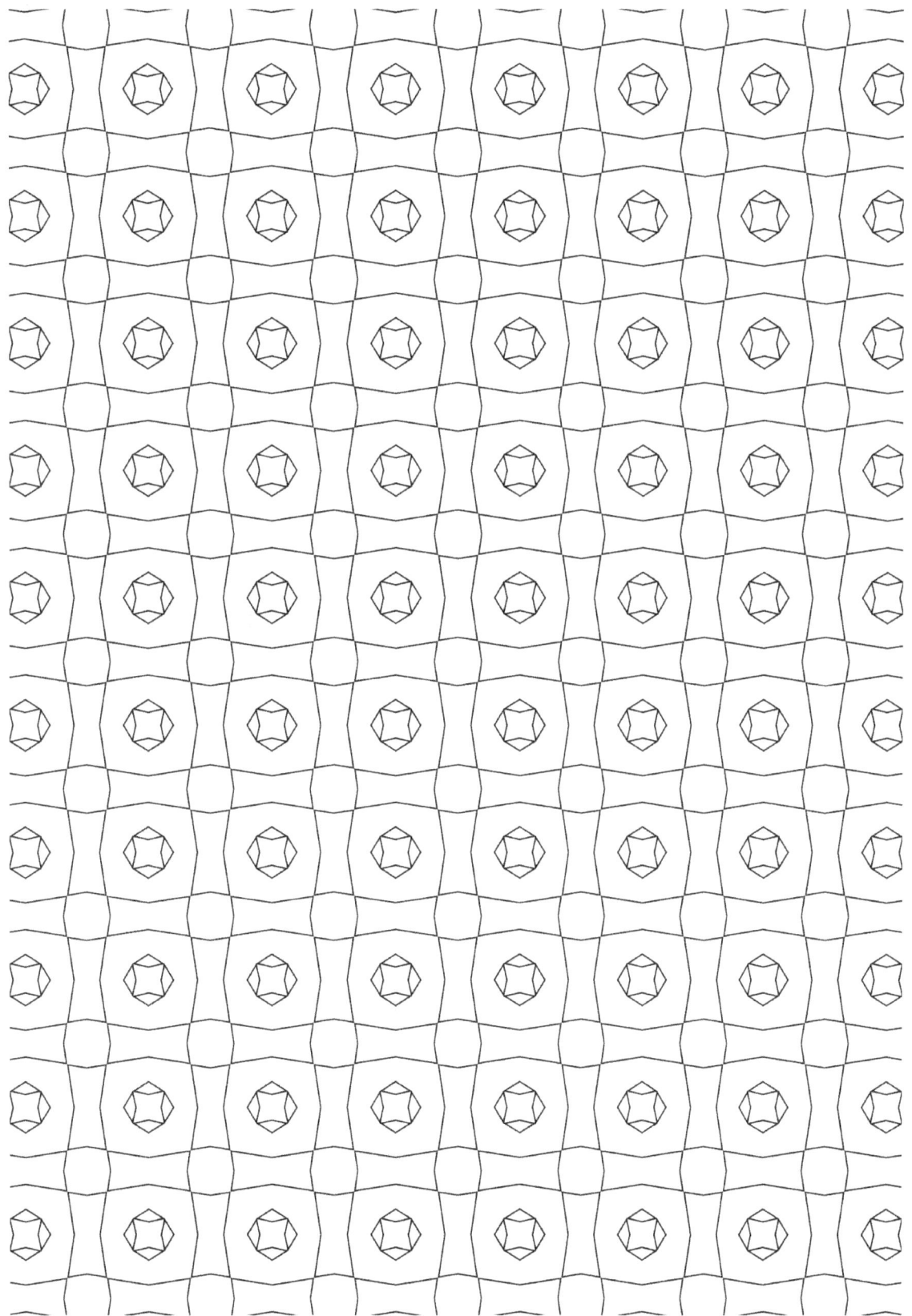

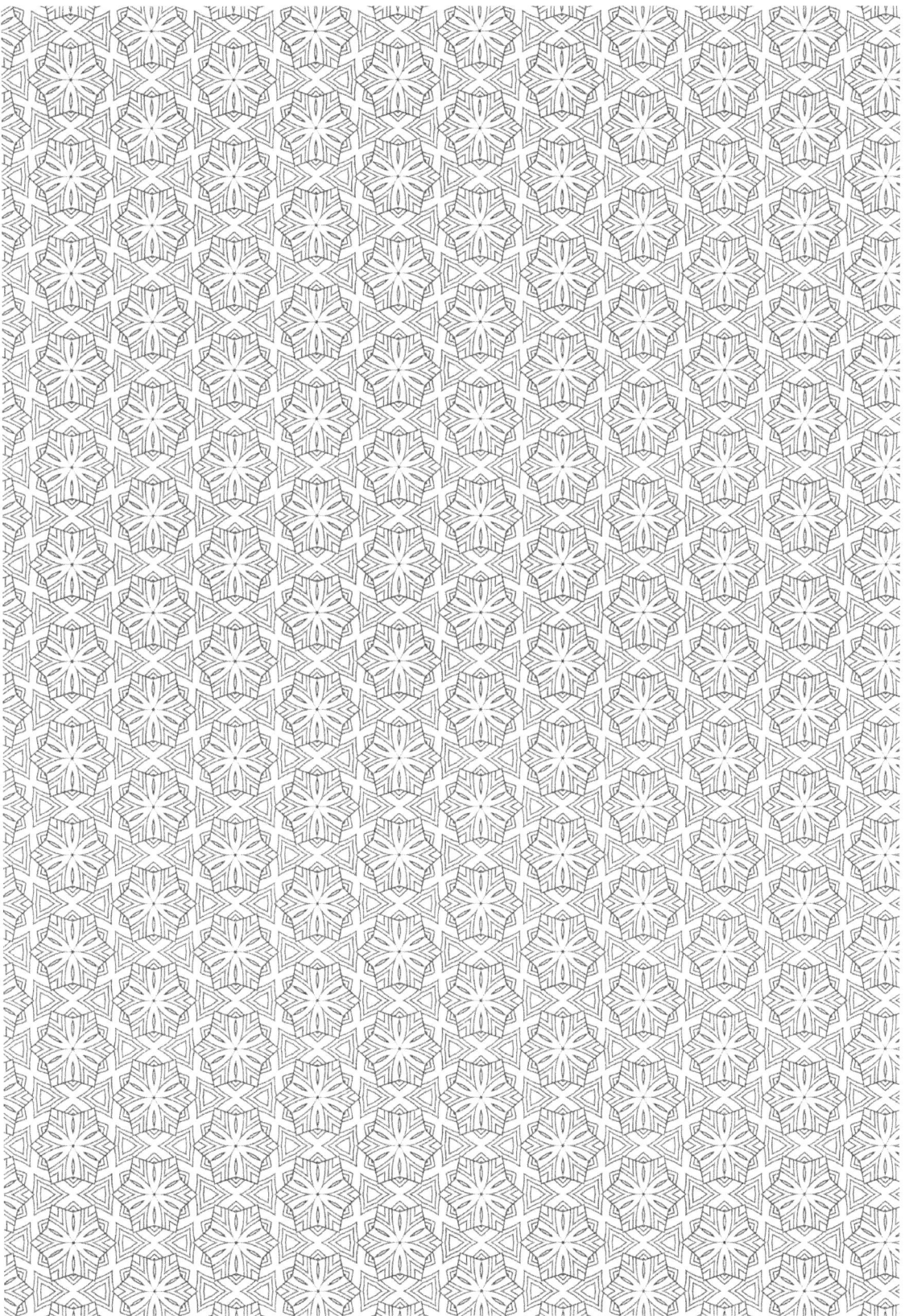

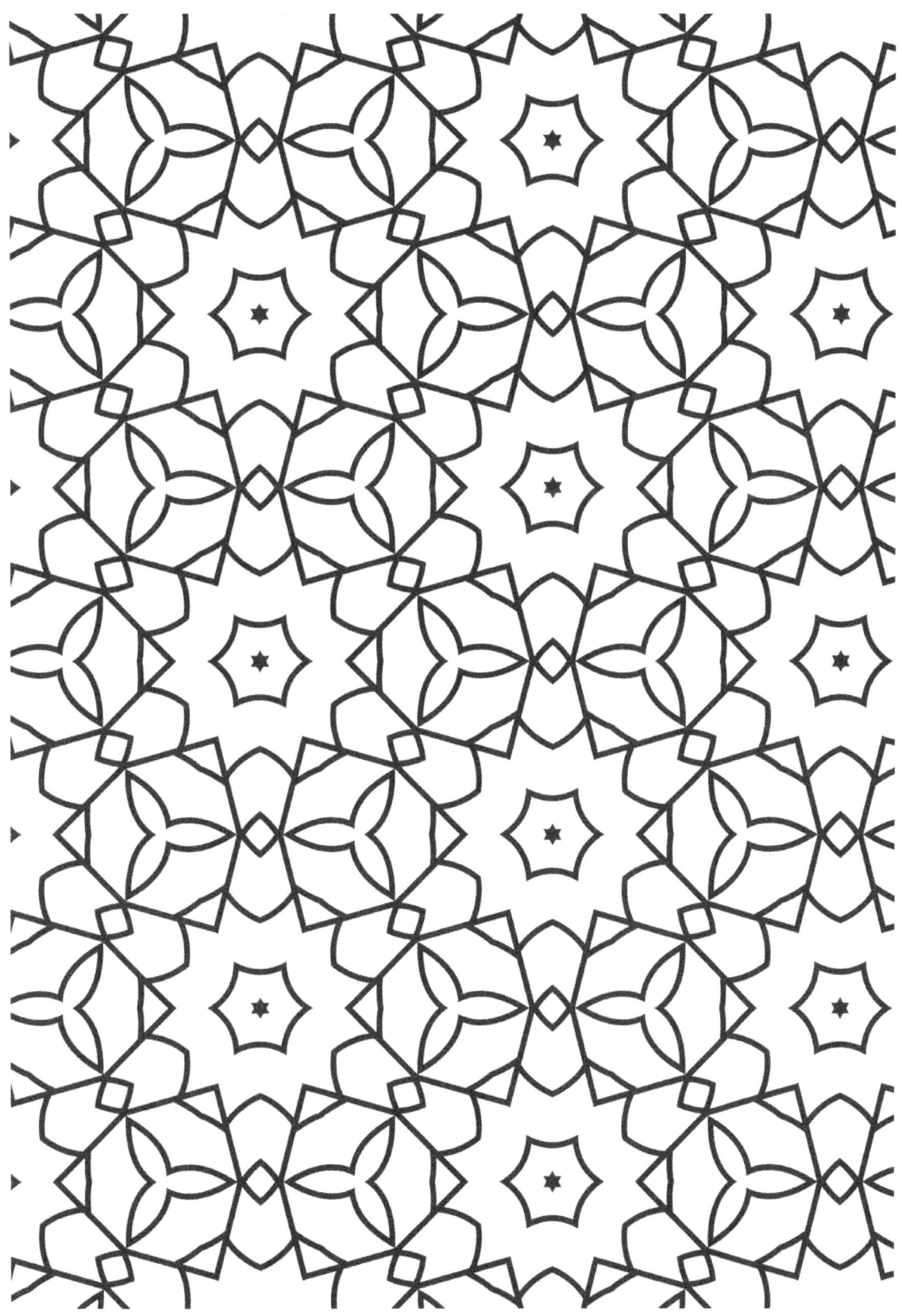

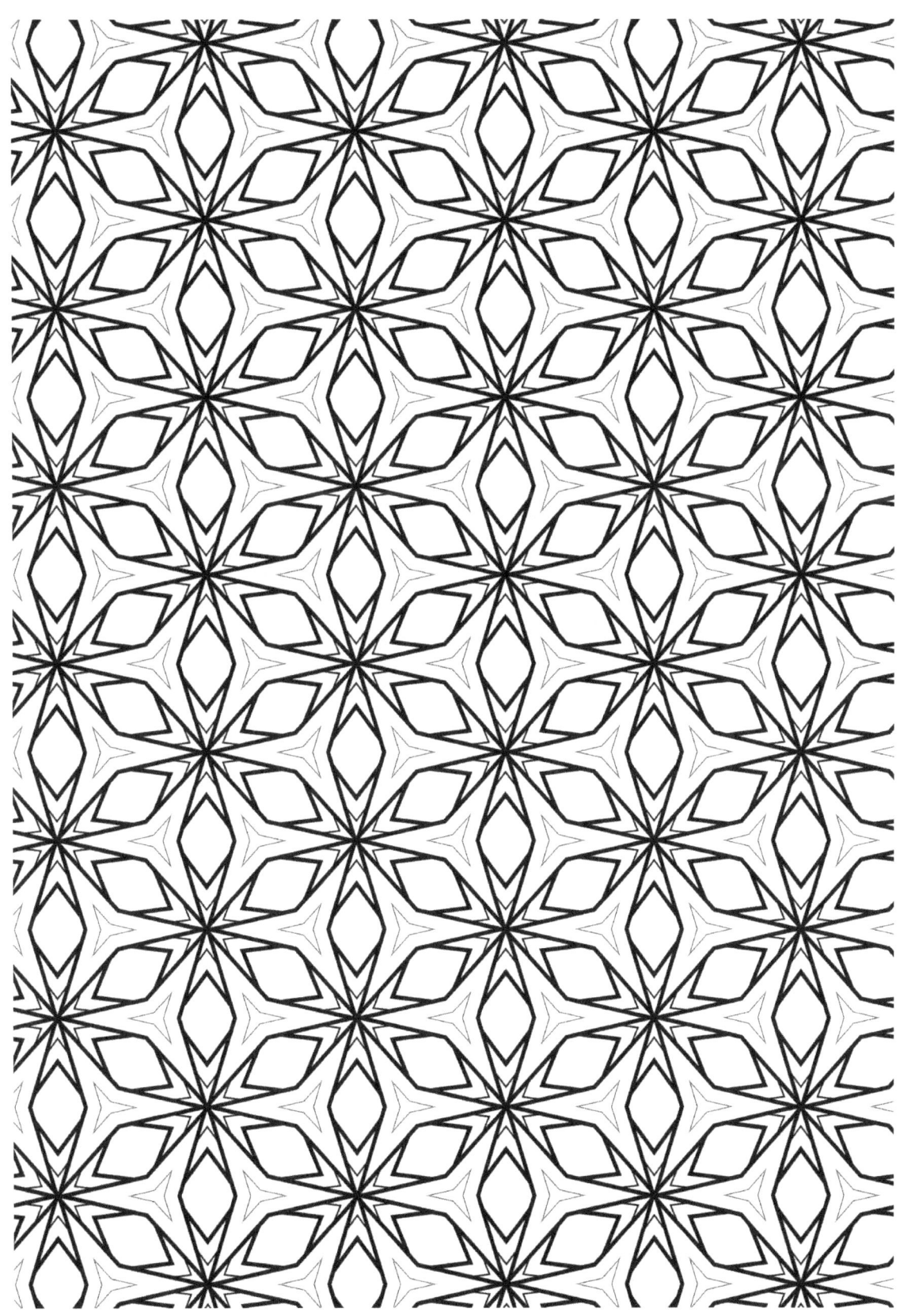

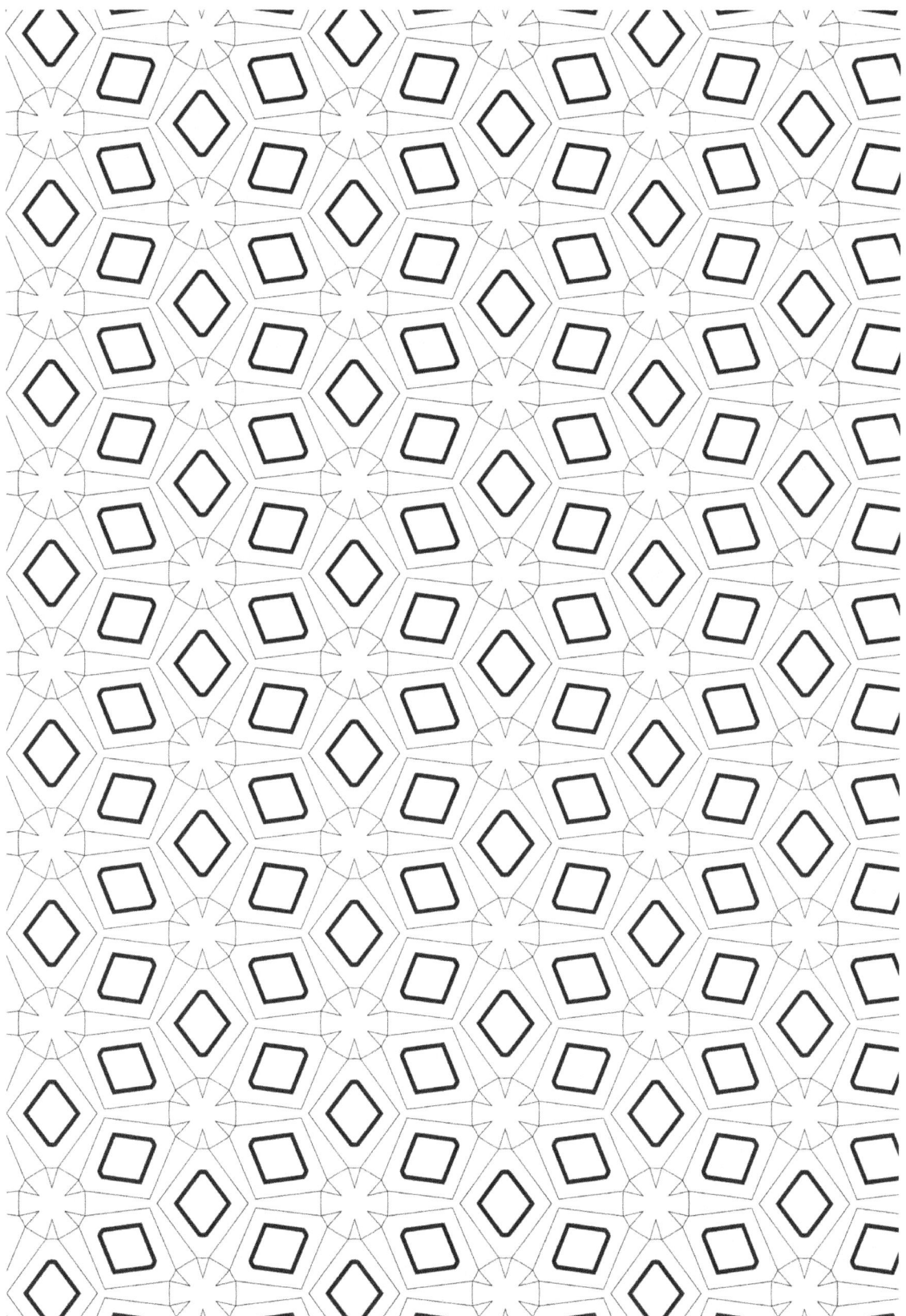

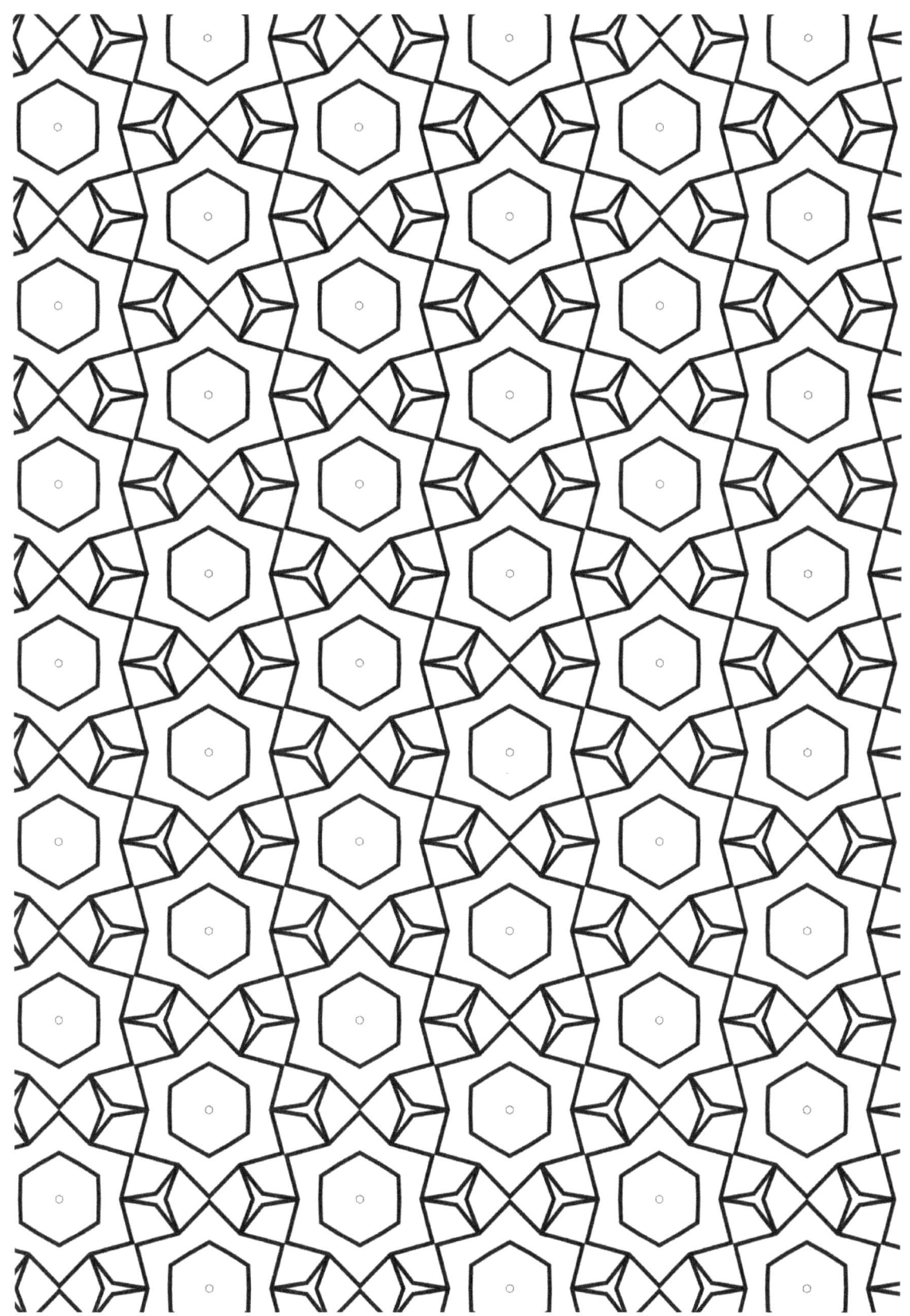

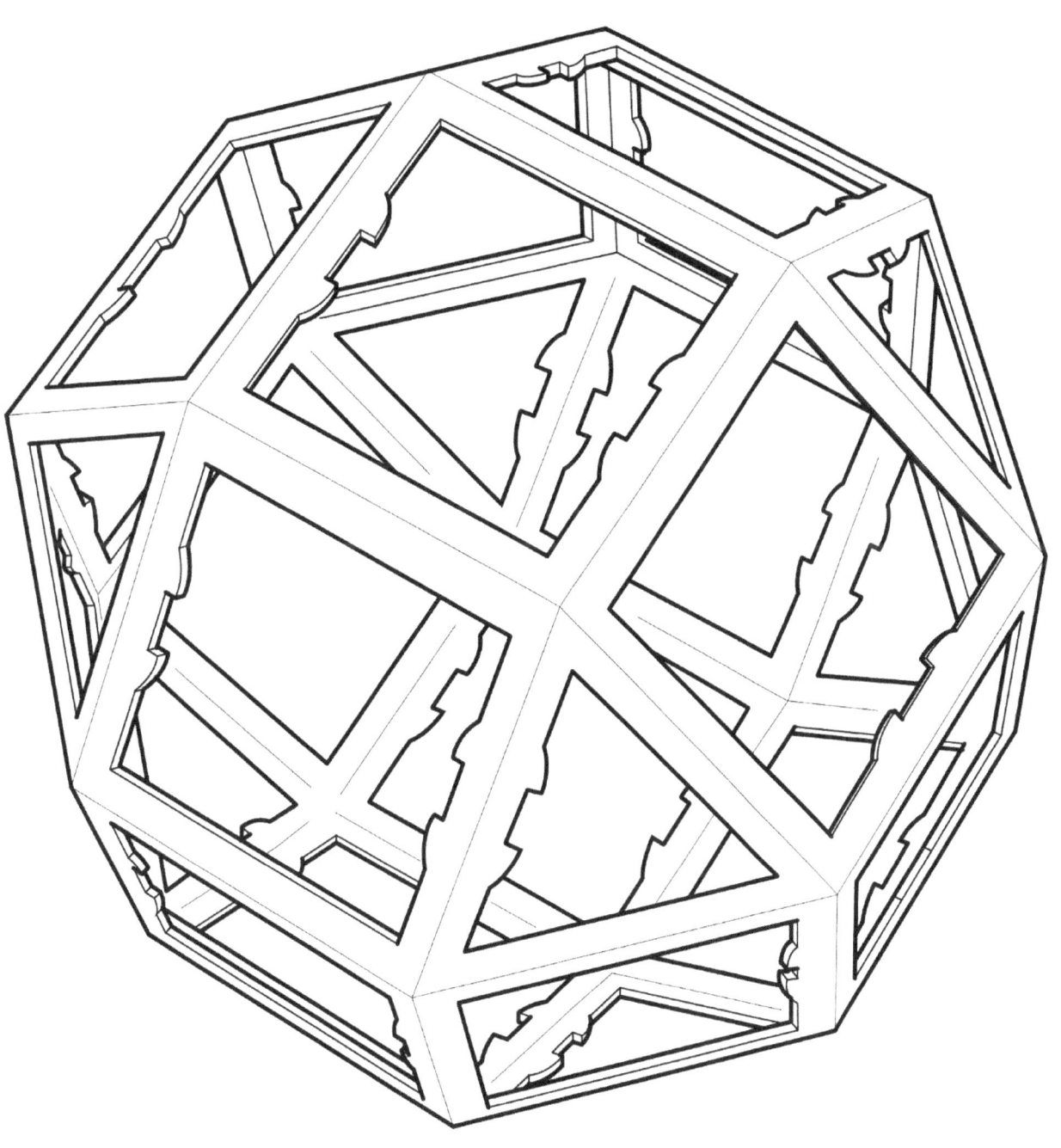

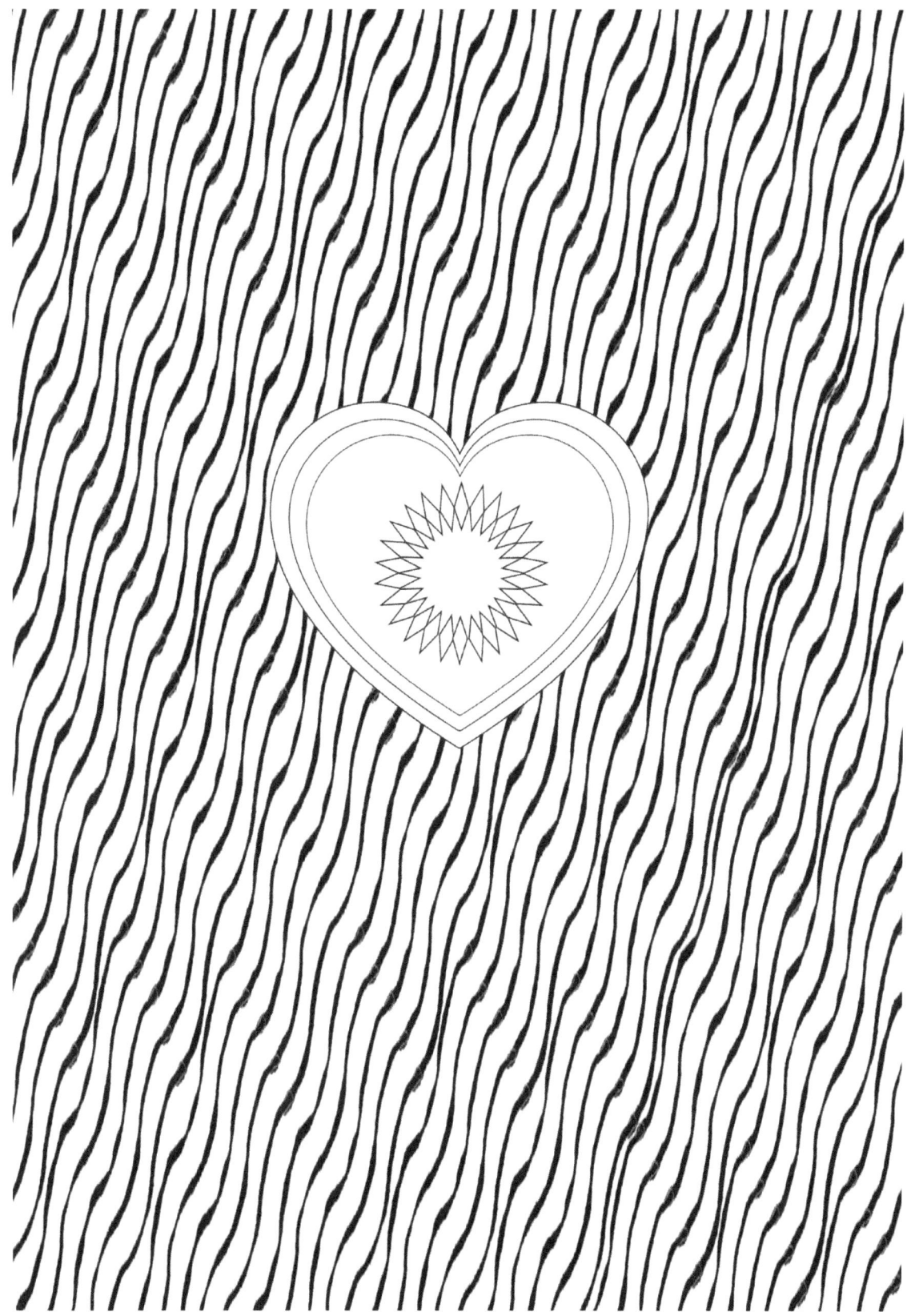

## THANK YOU AGAIN FOR PURCHASING THIS BOOK

Experiment with shading, colors and light to produce the effect that makes the best of the images and your artistic skills. I hope that you enjoy this book as much as I did creating it.

## Get a new coloring image each week for FREE

Come and join our Facebook page for help, tips and advice about getting the best from your coloring. Each week we release a new, exclusive, image that you can download and print out. You'll also be the first to hear about new coloring books that we release along with special discounts.

Join us at https://www.facebook.com/**adults**coloring**books**/

www.ingramcontent.com/pod-product-compliance
Lightning Source LLC
Chambersburg PA
CBHW080829180526
45168CB00006B/2617